A VILLAGE CHILDHOOD

By John David Beckett

Cover Photo: Pat, Laurie, David in Haxton Lane 2003
'The Last of the Summer Wine'

ISBN 9963-9226-0-0

Published by

J & P Books
E-mail sunbirds@waitrose.com

Printed By

FIRST EDITION: 2006 by Master Print,
Demetriades Bros Ltd: 1A Alsoupoleos Str.,
P.O.Box 40768,
Tel.: 357+24+635950, Larnaca, Cyprus
E-mail: Masterpr@logos.cy.net

ACKNOWLEDGEMENTS

I first thought of writing this book many years ago. I did in fact commence writing short extracts some years ago, and sent them to my two partners in crime. They said they enjoyed them, as did their families, but the items relied on my single memory. Other duties intervened, not the least being supervising the building of a house.

Whilst on a recent visit to Bratton I met Bob Shadbolt in the White Hart. He displayed interest in my memories and having read some of my earlier attempt, encouraged me to continue writing. On re-reading my earlier work I found, not only that the style was facile, but also that it contained numerous inaccuracies. I have therefore had to re-write everything, but I have Bob to thank for getting me started again.

My wife, Penny, not only put up with me monopolising the main computer with my one finger typing, but also got me out of the problems I encountered with the infernal machine. She also slogged away at proof reading and correcting my grammar.

I am deeply indebted to Pat and Laurie

who assisted my ageing inaccurate memory with theirs. Laurie particularly, as he struggled through the whole book, checking the anecdotes and supplying some of his own. He also provided many of the photographs.

I am extremely grateful to them all and hope they enjoy the final result.

DEDICATION

To all the villagers, past and present, who made our childhood such a magical experience.

CONTENTS

A VILLAGE CHILDHOOD

Preface

This is a factual book not a book of facts. By that I mean none of the writing has been researched. All incidents and descriptions are from the memories of three old men alone and that is a very fallible source.

Anyone requiring an accurate account of the history of Bratton Fleming and its buildings, the school, church or surrounding countryside I would recommend to read one of Terry Squire's meticulously researched volumes, or other such.

This is merely the recollections of a short time in the history of Bratton as seen through the eyes of a small boy. Although I have tried to remember names, places, persons and events, and have checked these, where possible, with my contemporaries, Pat and Laurie, they are only as we remember them and quite possibly not as they actually were.

Many places and names may be mis-spelt as we never saw them written down and our memories are confused, not only by their pronunciation in dialect, but also by the passage of time. I fear that certain passages might not be 'Politically Correct' today, but we were unaware of the term in those days and I have tried to give as authentic an account as possible.

Unfortunately it has been impossible to locate any contemporary photographs of certain places or people. Some of those included, therefore, pre or post date the era, and some are even modern, included to show the location of places referred to in the text.

Some of the practices described are today illegal, or will be at best thought barbaric. Readers should remember that it was not only a different age, but concerned a countryside population that had developed its own moral code, in isolation from the rest of England, especially the towns.

My object in writing this book is to record a period in Bratton's history, as memory serves, when, as Laurie once said, "We lived in a Time Warp".

I hope, in doing so, I have not engendered any ill feeling from persons portrayed who may be still living, or any descendants of those mentioned. If I have, I apologise unreservedly as that was not my intention.

I have tried to amuse the reader, as

well as record events. To the best of my recollection all the events described happened in the way they are described, but I would not vouch for their chronological order being accurate.

I hope the reader will accept the above explanations and enjoy the book in the spirit it was written.

Chapter 1

Croydon

I was born in Thornton Heath, Croydon on 28th August 1935. Christened John David, I was always referred to as David until the age of eighteen. I had an elder step brother Rex, and an elder step sister Beryl. I also had a younger sister Elizabeth, but she was always very sickly and died as a baby. I was a very frail child also, and could not take any fats. I mainly existed on vitamin tablets and peptonised milk, apart from sweets.

Before we moved to Devon my mother first asked the doctors opinion as to whether it was advisable for me. He told her it would be the best thing, and to take me down to the country air and "Let him run wild". I was certainly to do that.

I was not the most tractable of children and at an early age displayed the sort of behaviour that I was later to develop. Mother was talking to another lady on the pavement one day when the lady exclaimed "Good gracious is that your son?" Mother looked up to see me swinging in and out of the bedroom window on the curtains.

When my mother took me shopping

she had to keep me on reins. My favourite trick was to escape her control, whilst she was making a purchase, and hide, watching her panic stricken search for me. I also used to hang back when walking along the pavement with her and then disappear into a shop doorway to see the same effect.

My mother always replied with the truth to any of my questions about life. This surprised the doctor on a visit, when he playfully prodded my tummy button and said "What's this?" I replied "That's where I was joined to my mummy when I was inside her". He said, "Good God, I was at medical school before I knew that".

When I was two years old, still in Thornton Heath, three things happened which I can remember. Firstly Father started to take me to his garage with him and I showed a great interest in car mechanics, I also demonstrated that I was in love with grease and dirt.

If any customer complained of a noise from under their car the mechanics would immediately ask me to investigate as it saved them from jacking up the car, there being no hydraulic lift available and the inspection pit being normally in use.

I loved crawling around under the

vehicles and was adept at recognising a leaking exhaust, worn Hardy-Spicer Joint or broken springs. I loved those days at the garage, especially watching gas welding and tyre cutting, this latter is not performed nowadays. Then it was the practice for tyre manufacturers to use much thicker rubber.

When your tyres became bald of tread you just visited your garage which would have had a machine to cut new treads in the remaining rubber. This covered the operator, and watcher, in sticky black rubber dust from head to foot, much to my poor mothers chagrin.

Mother used to dress me in white shirts, velvet trousers, white socks and patent leather shoes, none of which was really suitable for a garage hand, but mother had greater aspirations for me which accounted for the second event that year.

I started school, not nursery school but a proper school albeit exclusively for girls. What strings were pulled to get a revolting boy like me into a prim girls' school I do not know. Mother obviously thought the discipline might be what I needed. The school was on the London Road near the end of Whitehall Road, and called Rosedean. It has long been transformed into offices but I still possess my old metal cap badge with the name emblazoned across it.

Off to School

I was collected every morning by some of the girl pupils who took it in turns to mother me throughout the day. They taught me to play the cymbals in the school band, and by the time I was four I was demonstrating quite a talent for reading and writing. This has subsequently made me agree with the people who say that education should not start before the age of five as I certainly went backwards later.

The third event was the Christmas present of a tricycle, with this I became both the terror and envy of the street, tearing along the pavement at top speed ringing my bell and expecting all pedestrians to leap into the road at my approach.

I also now ventured around the bend in Broughton Road for the first time and met a group of other boys slightly older than myself who would willingly give me sweets for a go on my trike. I quickly demonstrated developing business acumen and soon established the maximum viable rate in sweets per ride, Mother meanwhile, who was a definite "No sweets before a meal" person started getting very worried over my apparent lack of appetite.

At weekends Father used to take us to Croydon aerodrome to watch the planes. I think it must have been then that Rex and I both decided we wanted to be pilots. On shopping trips we frequently went to

Kennards in Croydon which had a large toy department. Rex pestered Mother to buy him a Frog flying model aeroplane powered by elastic. I was later to inherit this when he was flying real aircraft.

We also went on at least one trip to London Zoo, I remember a large gorilla sitting quietly in his cage. A man started throwing lumps of earth at it to make it move. The gorilla ignored him until he started to walk away, when it grabbed a big handful of earth and dung threw it accurately to catch him with a mighty thump on the back of the neck. I do believe I saw the gorilla grin.

About this time a gentleman, by the name of Hitler, was making rumbling noises in Germany and it became apparent, especially to people who had lived through the First World War as had my parents, that another conflict was coming.

Father decided that the best course of action was to build an air-raid shelter in the garden in conjunction with the next door neighbour, a Mr Godbolt. Mother was not enamoured of the idea as it meant the destruction of her summerhouse at the bottom of the garden which, although Father promised to reinstate it, as she suspected at the outset, was never re-erected.

I delighted in the great hole that appeared amid the huge piles of earth that covered our lawn. Never a man to do things by halves and applying a factor of safety of ten, Father lined it all with concrete and roofed it with reinforced concrete.

I remember seeing old iron bedsteads etc. being employed as reinforcing and I am sure it would have withstood a direct hit from a nuclear weapon had such a thing been invented. It certainly, in its time, stood everything Hitler could throw at it including the V2 that took out the house behind. It was a refuge for my brother, who stayed on in the house, and several other families throughout the Blitz.

However that was all in the future. Mother still had her little green Austin Seven, and I at the age of three being an expert on cars used to wait until I heard the magic words, "We'll take the car". Whereupon I would race out to the car, take off the handbrake, switch on the ignition and pull out the choke, (in those days keys were normally left in cars, the criminal fraternity being very small).

This was to lead to problems later but at the time, being forbidden to actually pull the starter, mother deemed it safe enough. I would then move to the passenger seat and await the rest of the family with eager anticipation as a car ride was still an adventure. This practice was shortly to cause the whole family problems.

Chapter 2

A First View of Devon

In 1938 my father had a customer to his Garage 'S and Bs' ('Smith and Beckett's), in London, who desired a station wagon, quite a novelty in those days. However this gentleman, by name Mr. Williamson, wished to purchase one for use at his Guest House called 'The Barton', in North Devon and he wanted father to deliver it.

You must remember at that time North Devon was considered as remote from London as Italy is today, it was like talking of a foreign country and the prospect of actually driving that distance was unimaginable. Cars were not reliable for more than 100 miles, fan belts broke, suspensions collapsed, main drive shafts broke, tyres punctured and cylinder head gaskets blew with remarkable regularity.

Nearly all car owners belonged to the AA and made good use of the ubiquitous yellow motor cycles and sidecars. In those days the AA was on the side of the motorist, as accidents involving pedestrians or other vehicles were rare.

The only big worry was the police

stopping you for the purely technical offence of speeding. The AA man's salute as you encountered him on the road meant that there were no policemen along the road he had travelled.

However, Mr Williamson had asked father to obtain and deliver a station wagon to him and that's what Father did. But he was not going to waste a journey of those proportions, so the whole family clambered aboard the station wagon and headed west. This was the time that an unfortunate fact manifested itself.

I was prone to travel sickness. I was just three years old. We had previously visited Brighton and Bognor for holidays and on those journeys no problems had arisen but they were mere jaunts when compared to this mammoth trip. With an impatient father driving, my only way of getting him to cease this purgatory to me was to declaim in a loud voice that I wanted to go to the toilet. I think that over the next few years I was to become acquainted with every toilet on the A4 and A38.

We did however eventually pass Taunton and enter the wilds of Exmoor, arriving at Blackmore Gate and thence to Parracombe, at which point we stopped and asked directions. We were directed out of the lower end of the village down a cart track with the valuable comment that The Barton was only half way to Hunters Inn.

The extra information was added that it was past someplace that sounded like 'Kittytoe', although we could not really believe we had heard correctly. It struck me then and often since, when being directed by Devonians, that they must have some mystical awareness of when they were half way to some unknown landmark.

It also occurs to me that many of my readers may not have ever lived in the days when a Devonshire cart track existed so it will bear a little explanation.

Sheep tend to follow one another, rather like sheep in fact, and in doing so wear little tracks or sheep paths, the sheep also tend to walk on the level so an abundance of these tracks occur around the moor lands like physical contour lines. Man also likes to walk on the level and where these tracks follow his desired direction he makes use of them both on foot and horseback.

In time, horse and carts also follow these tracks which give rise to a three rut track, two deep by the wheels and one shallow by the horse. As the three ruts tend to be muddy and waterlogged, following pedestrians and sheep tend to walk between them thus keeping the whole track worn down and relatively free from vegetation.

These tracks, although eminently suitable for horses, carts, sheep, and pedestrians in Wellingtons, were somewhat less suitable for motorised transport, in the days before tractors. It was however down one of these tracks we were directed from Parracombe to the Barton.

We descended into more of a gorge than a valley, in fact in this part of the world what is called a 'Coombe' or 'Cleave'. The trees met overhead and the sides of the Coombe reached up to the sky leaving just a narrow strip of starlight overhead.

The track descended more and more steeply but there was no room to turn around. We slowed for a moment when someone said "What is that noise", and wound down a window but all we could hear was a regular thumping from the trees beside the track and a loud sound of running water. Although we did not know it at the time this was our first encounter with a 'Water Ram'.

We continued to descend, unavoidably, as there was nowhere to turn around in any case, but silence pervaded the station wagon. We passed a farmhouse set back on the right from the road, with the name 'Kittytoe' painted in white on the top bar of the yard gate. This gave us courage to proceed and in a short time lighted windows appeared ahead and a small wooden sign saying 'The Barton'.

We drew into the forecourt of a large farmhouse on the left, opposite a row of cottages on the right. Having switched off the engine we could hear the sound of a rushing stream and Mr. Williamson appeared, to guide us into the house.

After supper we were soon in bed but up early the next morning to explore. It was a marvellous place and marvellous countryside. After London there were absolutely amazing things everywhere we looked and adventures around every corner. At the bottom of the farmyard was the first stream I had ever seen and I lost no time wading into it and getting saturated.

There were green fields and cows, again a first for me since I had only seen them in picture books before, and I lost no time in getting acquainted and watching the milking. Then it was up the steep wooded hillside to explore and for the first time to smell the heady perfume of the ubiquitous bracken.

After lunch we walked down the valley

following the cart track, picking wild
strawberries from the hedgerow on the way,
until we reached the 'Hunters Inn'. This was a
lovely old hotel with a white front, criss-
crossed with blackened wooden beams,
diamond paned leaded windows, in a
picturesque setting at the bottom of the
valley. Our parents had a drink with the
owners, two old ladies, sisters, called Berry.

Hunters Inn

We children explored the extensive
gardens to the rear of the hotel and watched
the trout in the stream which flowed
alongside. In the distance we could hear the

sound of the sea and it was not long before we persuaded my parents to continue the walk, passing beside the hotel but this time with no path to follow.

We scrambled along, following the stream, initially through woods, which in spring would be full of bluebells, but eventually emerging into a clearer valley bottom. Father said that the stream was called the 'Heddon' and we were approaching 'Heddon's Mouth'. Sure enough as we rounded a curve in the hillside the sea suddenly appeared, and a small pebble beach bisected by the river was visible.

Short but steep cliffs, gouged out of the valley sides surrounded the beach. On the left as we approached there was a large ruined stone structure, which initially we took for a ruined castle and treated it as such in our subsequent games. It was much later that we were told it was a ruined limekiln.

We passed a pleasant afternoon at Heddon's Mouth returning tired and happy to the Barton for supper and bed. I had decided by then that there was no way I was going to live my life in London but wanted to stay in that particular part of Devon for ever.

Even Eastbourne paled into insignificance beside the delightful countryside. Although our stay there was only to be a few days, none of us realised how soon my wishes would be fulfilled. A few days later we returned to London by train, Mr. Williamson having taken us by car to Barnstaple where we caught the train to Taunton, Bristol, and so to Paddington and home to Thornton Heath.

Chapter 3

Return to Devon

After our return to London events progressed as before, with me continuing to attend Rosedean School. We made one more visit to the Hunters Inn valley to deliver yet another car to Mr. Williamson after the first had succumbed from a diet of too many cart tracks. We found we were still enamoured with the beautiful countryside.

Then came the first practice air raid when war was declared. We had all been briefed by Father as to what we should do when the siren sounded. Father happened to be away that evening, however as soon as I heard the siren I leapt out of bed and ran into Mothers room where I climbed onto her back and locked my arms around her neck for a piggyback down to the shelter.

This caused her some consternation as she had not got her dressing gown on by this time. I refused to let go and begged her to hurry down to the shelter as Father had said we must. My brother Rex was trying to get us to hurry and my sister was in tears and shouting that we were all going to die.

We finally made it down to the shelter

with some confusion, where we met our neighbours who had come in through their entrance. We spent a miserable night in the cold and dark smelly confines of the shelter. How the residents stood it during the Blitz is beyond my imagination.

When Father got home he asked Rex how it had gone. Rex told him that it was absolute chaos and that if it had been the real thing he feared for our lives. It was therefore decided that we should leave London for the time being and the obvious place where we had a connection was North Devon. Father contacted Mr. Williamson and ascertained that there was an empty house available for rent at Trentishoe, above Hunters Inn.

We packed clothes and essentials into Father's Chrysler and Mother's Austin Seven, and with Father and Rex driving, we bade goodbye to Broughton Road. Father and Rex would be returning, Father to carry on with the garage or close it down, if the war so dictated, Rex to complete his apprenticeship in engineering at the Monotype. For the rest of us we were not to see Thornton Heath again until 1945.

We had told our next door neighbours, the Godbolts, what we were doing and they decided that Mrs Godbolt and her daughter

Lorna, who was my age, would come and stay with us in Devon, Lorna would come with us and her Mother would follow. So once again it was 'Westward the Wagons' and off down the A4.

We arrived in the Hunters Inn valley as it became dark and collected the keys to the house from Hunters Inn. It was then we found that the house was not furnished and we would have to sleep on the floor that night. We wended our way up the footpath to the house and discovered that it had not been occupied for a very long time, except by rats that had left much evidence of their presence.

We also discovered that there was no running water and that this had to be collected by bucket from the stream across the road and through the woods. Although we children looked upon it all as a great adventure Mother refused to stay there even for one night, so back we went to the Hunters and civilisation.

The next morning after much discussion it was determined that there was only one other property available in the valley. This was a bungalow in the grounds of the farmhouse called Kittytoe, a little way back up the valley past the Barton. We visited it and, although there were no cooking facilities, and again no water, which had to be brought from a stream just across the road, at least it was furnished to a standard acceptable to Mother so we moved in.

To us children it seemed like paradise tucked in as it was under a bracken covered hill, which ran down to one side of the bungalow and on the other wild woodland with a stream. The bungalow no longer exists, it was converted to a garage some years later and has since been demolished.

Kittytoe farm itself gained fame later as the home of Dave Allen, the comedian. Father and Rex, having at last got us settled, beat a hasty retreat back to the smoke and left us to fend for ourselves.

On our first day there I had my first adventure. Mother decided that we must go shopping in Lynton for food. On hearing this I made a quick exit.

Now, whereas in Thornton Heath the car was always parked on a level road outside our house, the bungalow at Kittitoe was perched on steeply sloping ground. This ran down past an adjoining woodshed to a single strand wire fence guarding a drop of about ten feet to the front of the farmhouse proper. Ensconced in the driving seat of the Austin I let off the handbrake.

My mother, realising what was happening, came flying out of the bungalow to see the car start moving off, she grabbed the spare wheel that was strapped onto the rear of the car but it was impossible for her to hold it on such a slope and she shouted out "Steer it David, steer it".

I grabbed the steering wheel, and as the fence approached swung the wheel to the right and turned into the woodshed, mother by this time had started shouting "Brake, brake" so I reapplied the handbrake and came to rest neatly parked in the shed.

However I vividly remember as I entered the shed that a farm worker was chopping firewood inside, his head turned towards me and as the car approached him, driverless as far as he could see, as my eyes scarcely cleared the dashboard, he threw the chopper one way and himself the other.

After the excitement had died down Mother decided we would set off for Lynton, but now came the problem, this was the late summer of 1939 and I had just celebrated my fourth birthday, and even rascals of that age have certain fears. I refused point blank to get into the car again, I had really traumatised myself. When I was finally forced into the car, in tears, I spent the whole trip screaming

"Look out, look out, we are going to crash".

Mother was at her wits end and when Father came to visit us explained the problem to him. He made me sit on his knee while he freewheeled the car from the bungalow to the woodshed several times.

He then made me steer it, still sitting on his knee, and operate the handbrake. Then I had to do the same again but with him sitting beside me. Finally he sent me solo and I lost my fear, so I learnt to drive when I was just four, albeit without the assistance of an engine.

On Fathers return to London he was accompanied by the Godbolts who had decided the wilds of Devon were too primitive for their tastes. I on the other hand was in seventh heaven.

No restrictions, being allowed to run free over the bracken covered slopes and walk to Hunters where we had our main meals, as there were no cooking facilities in the bungalow. We would play in the Hunters gardens until summoned by the dinner gong into the lovely dining room with fresh napery, a crusty roll on the side plate, and a steaming bowl of soup.

The walk to Hunters and back meant the gathering of wild strawberries from the side of the track. We used to light a fire outside the bungalow and cook a few things ourselves, getting water from the stream opposite. Many happy days spent at Heddon's Mouth climbing the sides of the cleave, with Mothers warning shouts of "Be careful up there". Anyone who has seen these steep precipices will understand her agitation but we had no fear of heights.

Heddon's Mouth

I do remember making myself useful on one occasion, being hauled out of bed at about nine p.m. one summer evening to explain to the female side of the family how to change a punctured wheel on the car. Where to place and how to use the jack, how to remove the hub cap and use the wheel brace, so my training at the garage came in useful at times.

As autumn drew on the bungalow became uninhabitable, the walls were only thin and it had no fires or heating so we moved into one of the cottages opposite The Barton. Mr Williamson had taken over Hunters by this time and was teaching me to ride his pony. There were beautiful woods behind the cottage and we explored them thoroughly. One day in a clearing we saw, curled up in the centre, a large animal.

We had no idea what it was but danced around the edge of the clearing hoping to get it to move. Eventually when it would not get up, and being too frightened to approach it, we went down to The Barton and described this huge black beast that inhabited the woods. A workman accompanied us back with a shotgun but when he saw it he laughed his head off and told us it was a dead Badger he had shot last week. We were still townies and had a lot to learn about the flora and fauna of the countryside, but it would all come over the years.

Chapter 4

The Move to Bratton

As winter drew on even the cottage at The Barton lost its appeal to Mother as it was really a summer let, so we started to look for alternative accommodation. Also my sister needed to attend school and that was quite difficult from the valley. Coming back from Barnstaple one day, with my visiting father driving, we were passing through Bratton Fleming when we saw a sign "House to Let". Father stopped the car and we had a look around Craigside from the outside.

After some inquiries we visited the owner, Mr Heal at Westland near Friendship and took Craigside on a long lease. I was mortified at moving into the village, I had loved the time in Hunters valley and could not believe that anywhere else could hold so many delights. However I had no say in the matter and we duly moved.

All our furniture arrived from Thornton Heath courtesy of Padfields, and my cousin June Stanbridge arrived from Horley, courtesy of her mother who thought she would be safer in the country. June was to live with us for the early war years.

Craigside today

Craigside in those days was a lot different to the house and grounds today. There was, and still is, a wide drive from the entrance gate round to the paddock gate but there the resemblance ceases. As the rest of my formative years were spent in this house and lands, a rather detailed description is fitting.

The top half of the front garden was down to vegetables and surrounded by apple trees, whereas the bottom was flowers with a holly tree in the corner by the wash house wall.

The front door led into a glass roofed porch or conservatory with shelves where we used to ripen apples and tomatoes. Inside the main house door was a small hall facing the stairs.

On the right was the FRONT ROOM, this deserves capitals as for many years it was only used on state occasions, except when inhabited by 'Paying Guests', of which we had many. It had a three piece suite and dining room suite and the piano on which my mother played at Christmas and other festive occasions. There was a fireplace and wall cupboard but of course no form of lighting.

On the left of the hall was the dining room, again with fireplace and wall cupboard but this room had a central gas light supplied by a Calor gas bottle under the stairs.

We all became adept at changing the bottles but I think the Health and Safety people would not approve of our method of checking the connection for leaks with a match. We never had any problem though. A leak was indicated by a small flame and we just tightened the connection until the flame was extinguished.

In this room we also had one of the few telephones in the village. The numbers were easier to remember then, ours being Brayford 202. I suppose that related to all the telephones for many miles around the

Brayford exchange, I wondered who had number 1.

Through into the kitchen, also gas lit, which had a window seat and an inglenook fireplace, complete with bread oven but in which now reposed the Bodley stove. This, together with a small gas stove in the scullery was going to become well known by Mother in her cooking efforts. The Bodley was lit by coal, coke, wood, whatever could be obtained at the time. Besides requiring a liberal and frequent application of Zebra black lead its chimney needed regular attention.

At that time there were two local ways of sweeping chimneys. One was to tie a stone to the end of a piece of binder cord and a furze bush onto the other. Throw the stone down the chimney and pull hard. The result was quite exciting but not as much as the other method. This consisted of poking the barrels of the double barrelled shotgun (of which nearly every household had at least one) up the chimney, and firing both barrels simultaneously.

This was warranted to work, unfortunately I was never to see either method in operation as Mother preferred the more prosaic method of getting Charlie

Marshall to come with his brush set. At least I had the excitement of seeing the brush come out of the pot and learning new swear words when he could not get it down again. I do remember him having to climb on the roof on one occasion and pull the lot upwards.

The scullery possessed a stone sink but no running water. From here led the back door, the door to under the stairs, and the door to the inner and outer larders. These last were large flagstone floored rooms with slate shelves around them supported by brick pillars. Strangely in the first larder there was also a water closet, this being supplied by rainwater off the roof.

No fridges in those days, as no electricity, so the larders were our cold rooms. Here the chicken eggs laid in summer were preserved, in water-glass in large pans, for winter consumption. Here also were the large pans of scalded milk placed to cool and form clotted cream, of which we always had a plentiful supply, passing the excess over the hedge to Mrs Holmes who turned it into lovely yellow butter and passed it back.

Upstairs there were three bedrooms, two double and one single. The two doubles were equipped with the standard wall cupboards and of course fireplaces. These fireplaces came into use when it was very cold in the winter or when anyone was sick.

To anybody who has not gone off to sleep in a room warmed and lit by firelight, watching the dying embers, I can tell them they have missed one of life's magical experiences.

On the other hand I can well remember, much later, being in the boarding school sickbay with mumps, after lights out, with the room lit by a flickering fire, listening to Valentine Dyall, (The Man in Black) reading 'The Beast with Five Fingers' on the radio. I will readily admit that I have never been so scared in my life.

But I get a long way ahead of myself. The window of the single bedroom overlooked the Alms houses and part of the graveyard. As it was to be my room my mother covered the window panes with sticky backed translucent paper so I could not see the graves. I remember I protested that she was shutting out God's garden but it cut little ice with her.

Also upstairs we had something very few other houses in Bratton had, a bathroom. The bath and basin were equipped with hot and cold taps but only the cold ones were connected, and these to a large rectangular tank which protruded into, and took up half the ceiling of, the bathroom.

This water tank was fed from the roof gutters and was the only source of water in the house, also supplying the bathroom toilet. What unimaginable detritus collected in this tank we never knew but we brushed our teeth in the water from it.

I, being small and normally dirty, sometimes had the dubious privilege of using the bath with a few inches of cold water supplemented with a kettle full of hot. From the bathroom window I later found it was possible to jump across the intervening space and land in the Alms house hedge, which provided a useful avenue of escape when sent to my bedroom.

The remainder of the house apart from the dining room and kitchen was lit at night, in common with nearly all the other houses, by oil lamps. These one had to carry from room to room, presenting difficulties if one person wanted to go to the toilet. If no candlestick was handy you had to fumble out in the dark or leave the other occupants lightless. We possessed many candlesticks and always went to bed by candlelight.

Imagine a young boy being left alone with a lit candle beside his bed nowadays,

Social Services would have something to say. I used to build camp fires of the dead matchsticks in the tray of the holder, stick dead matches into the soft grease beside the wick as an extra wick etc. It is a wonder that I never set the house on fire.

Later we had a bulb holder attached to the top of an acid accumulator, which Fred Ewens would recharge, and used these instead of candles. In my case this was an improvement as I could then read under the bedclothes when sent to bed, liquid acid under the bedclothes!!

Later we acquired an Aladdin oil lamp. This gave a much better light in a room than the standard oil lamp, enough to easily read by without straining your eyes. Although not pressurised, it used a mantle to burn the oil instead of a wick, and gave a lovely soft light.

Later still we progressed to Tilleys but in some ways, although they gave a much brighter light they were a retrograde step as the persistent hissing noise got on ones nerves. Torches, although very useful, especially for visits to outside privies, were used economically as batteries were hard to come by.

Outside the back door was a small concreted yard, with a path between two flower beds leading to a brick built earth closet which we later changed to a WC. Leading off the yard was the wash house attached to the main building.

Rear of Craigside from Church Tower

This housed a mains water tap which we almost immediately had extended to the kitchen via a lead pipe under the yard. This pipe froze and burst many times each winter and I spent many happy hours watching it being dug up, repaired with solder and reburied.

I think our water came from Castle Moor reservoir and, although we rarely had tummy trouble, Mother always kept a piece of muslin tied over the tap and frequently emptied it of fresh water shrimps and other nasties that came down the pipes. The rest of the wash house contained the log store, coal store, animal feed bins and of course the copper and mangle which gave it its name.

A tall door (to stop chickens flying in) led from the yard into the large paddock. On the right were a partly enclosed Dutch barn and a smaller shed where we would keep first the trap and later, when that was disposed of, the car.

On the opposite side of the paddock was the drive gate, next to it was a faggot pile for our firewood. At the bottom of the paddock was a large hen house, which I hated in years to come as it was always my job to give the inside its annual coat of lime wash and get infested with chicken fleas at the same time. Next to that was the pig sty and close by, a two cow shippon and feed store.

A shippon was where the cows were housed over the winter and brought into when needing attention in the summer. They were frequently just wooden structures covered in galvanised corrugated iron with often just an earth floor although ours was concrete.

Milking was carried out in the shippons in those days and it was not until the end of the war that rendered concrete block TT milking parlours started to appear which were much more hygienic.

The roof gutters of the shippon carried water into a large wooden butt, the contents of which were used to wash out the shippon after milking. I used to be told off for hanging over the butt as Mother said it contained Diphtheria. On the hedge beside grew a large Crab Apple tree, the fruit of which I tried to eat each year but the taste never got any better.

Through the gate from the paddock was a big field which stretched along the bottom of the churchyard and way beyond. Past the end of the churchyard was a brick built cistern which was spring fed and never ran dry. This was the home of many newts, which we tried to catch with a bent pin on string, but with little success. Against the further hedge was a small pond also spring fed and in the bottom corner of the field a stream passed through.

This is now all buried under Furze Park estate, no wonder some inhabitants complain of damp houses. It was in this field we kept our cows, ponies, sometimes sheep, and made hay. But that was all in the future.

June and David on arrival at Craigside

Chapter 5

Early life in Bratton

Having moved in and got ourselves more or less straight indoors, we started on the outside acquisitions. At this time Father sold his interest in the garage and joined the Ministry of Supply as a Quality Control Officer of army vehicles, with an office in the County Garage in Barnstaple.

He was responsible for the standard of repairs in several garages such as Prideaux in Bear Street, The Central Garage on the square etc. all of whom were required, during the war, to repair a quota of varied mechanical contrivances.

I call them that due to the peculiarity of some of the amphibious vehicles, in addition to the more common Jeeps, armoured cars, Bren gun carriers, half tracks, Matador searchlight towing vehicles and others. All of which were parked in the drive of Craigside on occasions and which I had the fortune to ride in and even drive in the yard sometimes.

However, for the moment, Father decided that we must make use of the field, and also find a substitute for Mothers Austin, as petrol rationing precluded its use. In short order he acquired two cows, and employed Mr Mitchell from the Village Hall to tend and milk them. He bought two dozen chickens, a cockerel, and two piglets for the sty. Having equipped the animal sheds he bought a pony and trap for Mother. Quite a large pony called Blackie.

He then bought a pony called Brownie for my sister, a smaller one called Starlight for June, which I inherited later after her return to the city, and a little Shetland called Tiny for me.

Beryl & June with Brownie and Starlight

I think he had inflated ideas of how many animals our field could support and before he started buying our sheep we had to start renting more fields. In the meantime we possessed all this livestock, having recently come from the smoke where you only occasionally saw a dray horse apart from the animals in London Zoo.

I must say that all the locals were free with their advice. There did not seem to be so much of the "Why should I empty my head to fill yours," attitude among Devonians that later crept in when the invasion of townies became overwhelming.

I remember the struggle we had to harness poor Blackie to the trap the first time. There was a complete tangle of harness and bits to be connected. Between Mother, Beryl and June, assisted by unhelpful comments by myself, it was finally accomplished, as we thought correctly. We all then mounted the trap.

It was a lovely conveyance, all wood, with high wheels, a little door and step for gaining access at the rear, plush lined seats all the way around inside, and on the top of the mudguards it had acetylene lamps. Mother, of course we all knew, could turn her hand to anything, she was completely dauntless over any obstacle. Although she had not driven a trap since before the First World War she grasped the six foot carriage whip firmly, tapped Blackie on the rear and made a clucking sound. It worked, off we set up the drive and up the main road.

As we approached the White Hart there was a group of teenage boys standing outside the Smithy and their heads whipped round to stare at these two young girls who had arrived from foreign parts. June remembered Mother saying in an undertone, "Eyes front girls, do not look at them", so we drove past in stately silence clopping on our way.

No ribald comments followed us as would surely happen today. We proceeded up to the top of the village but when we got opposite what we eventually found to be Charlie Clarke's house a man stepped out into the road and said "Whoa Missus".

Mother bid him good morning proudly from her lofty perch but he continued, "You'm 'as got thicky there 'orses collar on upside down". Much shame amongst the female crew, and with welcome assistance from Farmer Steer, for it was he, the wrong was righted and we proceeded on our test drive to Sentry Cross before turning for home. I think Blackie was glad we did not attempt Grange

Hill with that load on board.

The trap served us well for many years, taking us to Barnstaple on market days as well as local journeys until it met its fate one day, some years later, near Chelfam Viaduct.

My sister was driving it by herself on the way to Barnstaple when from the other direction came a lorry full of soldiers. As can be imagined the sight of a teenage girl excited the troops and resulted in a loud chorus of whistles and ribald shouts. This was more than Blackie could stand and he bolted.

One wheel of the trap went up the bank and over went the whole contrivance scattering its component parts along the road. Beryl was thrown out, luckily with nothing worse than minor scrapes and bruises.

Fortunately the lorry stopped and a remorseful load of soldiery caught the horse and picked my sister up. I don't think she was too displeased to return home in the company of a lorry load of virile young men but that was the end of our trapping days.

In the early days at Craigside I was kept under fairly strict control and only ventured out into the village accompanied. When not riding Tiny adorned in jodhpurs complete with little riding crop, I was dressed as Mother thought befitted my station. Still white shirt, velvet shorts, white socks and strap over patent leather shoes.

Granted I tended to get them rather dirty as I was always around the animals in the paddock and in the shippon watching Mr Mitchell milk the cows, as he sat on the traditional three legged stool with his cap on backwards and his head pressed into the cows flank.

He taught me to milk as well and I loved to squirt the milk straight from the cow's teat into my mouth, who ever heard of pasteurised or TT tested in those days. Mr Mitchell was later christened Gandhi by Pat. I think Pat thought that when Mr Mitchell, with his bald head, sat on an upturned bucket in the shippon staring into space, which was how he spent most of his working time it seemed, he reminded him of the Indian mystic.

However, 1939 drew to a close with us firmly established at Craigside and the phoney war coming to an end. We celebrated our first Christmas in Devon in traditional fashion. We bought a goose from the Land's farm at Chelfham. We had the tree decorated with our old pre war decorations brought from London, and I do remember one item that would horrify people today.

These were little clip on candle holders which held miniature candles rather like birthday cake candles. They were clipped on to the branches of the tree and set alight on Christmas day. The fire hazard was beyond comprehension and surely no one would be insane enough to do that today, but there again nowadays everyone has electricity and uses fairy lights.

I think Mother had hoarded some crackers and rationing had not started to bite hard so we had an excellent family Christmas with Rex coming down from town.

Rex indulged in great arguments with Father as he wanted to break his engineering apprenticeship and join the RAF. Mother, having had brothers in the trenches in the first war was very anti-military. She said only fools joined the forces and "Better a live coward than a dead hero".

Rex being headstrong, as most youths, eventually a year or so later joined up of his own volition and was off to Canada for pilot training.

We had quite a snowfall around Christmas that year and I came down one morning to find a drift completely obscuring the dining room window.

It can snow in Bratton (1947)

From the time we arrived in Bratton my only desire was to be out of doors, as it had been at the Hunters Inn valley. Unlike most young boys I was not interested in food and my mother had great difficulty in getting me into the house for bed or even at mealtimes. I remember on one occasion she put me in the dining room, after much protestation, and sat me before a plate of fish and mashed potato, telling me I could not go out until I had finished it.

She was rather surprised to hear me call very soon, "It's all gone can I go out now". She looked in and seeing the empty plate allowed me out. When she went into the room to clear away she found fish and potato all over the walls. I had flicked it all around the room from the end of my knife. Retribution followed my return and I believe I was confined to barracks for a few days.

I was also in trouble when, after hearing Mother complaining about people looking in our front windows as they walked down the footpath through our drive, I constructed some man traps. I spent a long time digging huge holes. I had then covered them with twigs and hidden the lot under clats of turf. I told her that, after a few people had broken their legs, they would think twice before using the footpath. She made me fill them in pronto.

Chapter 6

Our Gang

One day in early 1940 I was sitting on the top of the gatepost at the end of our drive when a village urchin approached. He was clutching a paper bag and chewing something. I asked him what he was eating and he said birds' eggs and offered me one.

In the bag were sweets, ovoid in shape, covered with different coloured spots resembling little eggs. I took one and found it very tasty and asked him where he got them. It must have been from Lower Shop but he replied "Axen Lane", I later found out that the correct name is Haxton Lane but normally pronounced Axen by locals.

I had visions of many birds' nests full of these delightful sweets so I asked him if he would take me there. I climbed off my perch and accompanied him down the road, little did I realise that this was the start of a lifelong close friendship with him. He told me his name was Laurie Tribe and admitted that he was exactly six months younger.

His style of dress intrigued me as he had on a grey shirt, corduroy shorts, grey socks and massive hobnail boots that looked far too heavy for his skinny legs to lift. They made a fine noise of clashing steel on tarmac as we walked, and I noticed him keep looking at my strap over patent leather shoes with a kind of wonder.

We were so engrossed in telling each other about ourselves and our families that we forgot about birds' eggs, having finished the bag between us, and started walking down Haxton lane.

He revealed that he lived with his parents and elder brother George in his Gran's house, two doors above the butchers. They had recently arrived to live with her, from Dunchideock, where his Dad had worked as a gardener, but now worked in Barum for Rawle Gammon and Baker.

By the time we reached Buttle we knew most of each others history, Laurie had visited Bratton before so knew his way around to some extent. He certainly knew the delights of the field called Buttle which had three streams running through it.

We passed the remainder of the day damming streams and turning the water down over the field to the next stream and so on. It was perishing cold but our work kept us warm, although Laurie still says that all his time in Bratton, as a child, his knees were perpetually blue with the cold.

By the time our tummies determined it was about meal time we looked remarkably similar in dress. Both our shirts were covered in brown mud, my velvet shorts were the same brown as his corduroys as were our socks. The mud adhering to my little shoes had increased their size to compete with his hobnails. On our return to civilisation my Mother was not impressed by my appearance.

She did not appear to take much notice of my excited description of my day's doings and of the little friend I had met but rather concentrated on my state of cleanliness.

I think that was the first time I was bathed in the copper. Why it is called a copper I have no idea, as there is no copper metal involved. It is a square brick structure containing a fire grate underneath and a cast iron bowl above. The bowl is filled with water, the fire lit, and the clothes for washing inserted and boiled. In this case it was me not clothes, and although I was not boiled I was scrubbed pretty thoroughly much to the amusement of Beryl and June.

That evening there was a family discussion, in which I was not included, regarding the standard of my dress. I believe my corner was supported by Father, who always said Mother mollycoddled me.

This culminated in a trip to Barnstaple the following day where I was equipped with hardwearing grey shirts and socks, corduroy shorts and boots, these latter came to me via Bill Merrett who liberally studded the soles and equipped them with steel tips and cues, the tips being steel pieces at the front of the sole and the cues a horseshoe shaped piece of steel around the heel.

This uniform felt marvellous to me but it bid goodbye to a lot of Mothers aspirations for my appearance. The only thing I did not win on for a long time was the belt. Mother insisted that belts around the middle of growing boys were harmful and made me wear braces. I wanted the brown and yellow striped belt with the snake buckle that Laurie wore.

Thus attired, Laurie and I roamed the countryside and Mother became adept at mending the three cornered tears that we used to come home with, in shirt or shorts, most days. It must have been on one of these early excursions that we met Pat Parkhouse. As Laurie was six months younger than me so Pat was six months older.

This age difference made not the

slightest difference to us in those days but latterly it has taken on an unwarranted significance. At this moment in time Laurie is constantly reminding us both that we are in our seventies whilst he is still in his sixties, but he will not chuckle for long.

It is amazing how when you are very young you are proud of being older than someone else, but when you are old you are jealous of the younger. However I have leapt forward some sixty five years.

Pat & Laurie

Pat's family had arrived in Bratton from Burrington and consisted of two elder sisters, Brenda who unfortunately died in her teens, Kathleen and his elder brother Ivor, who worked in Prideaux's garage. Pat's father was a postman and covered the Challacombe area by bicycle in all winds and weathers each day.

Pat lived in the road behind the White Hart, next door to Freddie Shapland, who was slightly older than us. Although we played with Freddie a lot he did not always accompany us and one sad day when we all went to Loxhore Freddie stayed behind. He was promised a ride on the steamroller that was repairing the road by Loxhore Lane, as his father was working there.

Freddie was on the roller when he saw the foreman coming and, so as not to get the driver into trouble, he jumped off the back. Unfortunately he caught his foot in a chain and swung down hitting his head on the projecting, surface breaking spikes before falling under the rear wheel. The roller was in reverse and could not stop in time.

We arrived back from Loxhore at the scene just after it had happened and on asking one of the workmen if he knew where Freddie was we were told shortly to "Git along home", which puzzled us until we heard the sad news. All the school contributed to a memorial vase for his grave which is outside the rear door of the Church. Every time I visit Bratton now I always visit his grave and straighten the vase and remove any overgrowing grass.

Fred's Stone
Inscribed 'To Fred from teachers and schoolmates'

Pat on the other hand was a permanent member of our gang of four, the fourth we did not really meet until I started school on the same day as him, Raymond Bennett.

Raymond, or Buster, lived in the last house on the left hand side up Vicarage lane.

At least it was the last house before the council houses were built. Raymond's father was understood to be blind and always carried a white stick.

Pat remembers him commenting on some bullocks running down a field on the distant horizon by Stoke Rivers. Pat says his young eyes could hardly make them out, so we had our doubts on Mr Bennett's lack of eyesight. Although his family came from Buckinghamshire, Buster was the only one of us actually born in Bratton. However this did not make him a local, as we were always told you had to have grandparents buried in the churchyard before you could call yourself local.

Raymond's mother was dead so we always felt a bit sorry for him and did not rag him too much about his figure or his lack of agility in tree climbing, or ability in squeezing through drainpipes after us. Unfortunately Raymond became partially paralysed in the Polio epidemic in the late forties. He married and had children I understand, when he was working for W.H.Smiths in Plympton. He died quite young, but by then we had lost touch.

The four of us, Pat, Laurie, Buster and I formed the top of the village gang. We had temporary additions from time to time, John Dinnicombe who came from Loxhore, Gordon Ward who moved into Bratton later, and various evacuees. Michael Bunce and Michael Montague are two names I remember. Later there were also David and Curly Barrow who came to live down Station Road.

We four formed the stable nucleus though, and we four got the blame, not wholly undeservedly, for any nuisance caused in the village. We were fairly territorial, being constrained from extensive activities at the bottom of the village by the older resident gang there, consisting of Raymond and Gordon Lott, Derek Marshall and Raymond Squire.

The only one from that area who did not beat us up on sight was Raymond (or Ginger) Squire. His elder brother Ronnie even tolerated us getting in his way at harvest times when he was doing contract work and we all thought they were both great guys.

Ginger was to become the best Darts player in the village and hardly ever had to buy a round of drinks in the White Hart as a result.

I met Gordon Lott again, many years later when he was a policeman in Bristol.

Raymond Squire & Gordon Lott

Chapter 7

Haymaking at Craigside

In the spring of 1940 we made our first field of hay. When the weather had been fine for a few days at the end of May, so that the sun had dried off the undergrass to ground level, and it appeared set fine for the next few days, my father requested the contractor to come and cut the hay.

Next day the contractor arrived, coming down our drive with his horse pulling the Finger Mower, the blade of which would be locked vertical and its blade and fingers protected by a wooden channel. I followed him through our paddock and into the big field at the back, half of which we had laid up for hay, confining our two cows to the other.

On entering the field the blade was lowered to the horizontal, the gear to the wheels engaged and they, the man and horse, set off around the field in ever decreasing circles. The chattering blade sheared the grass off cleanly which then fell back across the bed to lie behind in a sweet smelling row.

The man plodded around behind the mower clutching the reins of the horse and keeping an eye open for mole hills, which blunted the blades, or mouse's nests which were balls of interwoven dried grass. These nests would lodge on the pointed mower fingers and flatten the grass ahead of the blade leaving a line of uncut grass.

To remove them, the horse was stopped and the man pulled off the offending nest. If the horse moved during this operation the man was in imminent danger of losing one or more fingers.

There was no chance of the grass drying and turning into hay whilst it lay in tightly packed rows. The few hay tedders which could be used to scatter it across the field were always in constant use by their owners and could not be spared. My mother, sister Beryl, cousin June and myself therefore, armed ourselves with pitchforks and moved across the field tossing the grass in the air to aerate and dry in the sun.

It was very hard work and we made frequent visits to the hedge where Mother had set a basket containing bottles of lemon squash. No sooner had we completed turning the whole field than it was time to start all over again.

Mother would leave us at lunch and tea time to return with a basket of food. We would pause thankfully and sit on the ripening hay to tuck into sandwiches and pies, washed down with cold tea or lemonade. After tea we had to prepare the field for the night.

To prevent the dew dampening all the hay and turning it back to grass it was normal to use a horse drawn, very long rake, called a Huxtable Hay Rake. This would be dragged around the field gathering up the hay, being raised every so often, leaving the hay piled in rows. Unfortunately these were also in use by their owners as every farmer was making hay at the same time, taking advantage of the weather.

We, therefore, had to use the different and more arduous system of 'pooking'. We had to use our pitchforks to rake up the hay and make big piles of it called pooks all over the field. I suppose the word originates from poking the hay up into piles, but whatever it was called it took us a long time and was very hard work. By that time my father was home and helping us but it was getting very late before we had completed 'pooking up' the whole field and the dew would be coming down.

The next morning it was back to the field again as soon as the sun had dried the dew off the 'pooks' and the short cut sward in between them. We set to, tearing down the 'pooks' and scattering the slowly drying hay out across the field again. The day was a repetition of the previous one.

Round and round the field turning the hay with pitchforks. The sun was rarely strong enough to make the hay in two days although it felt very hot when one was working so hard, 'pook' it up again that night and retire at least secure in the knowledge that if it did not rain we should be getting it in on the morrow.

The third day we again spread it out and turned it but started putting it into heaps immediately after lunch. Then mid-afternoon the contractor re-appeared with his horse and cart. He plodded around the field stopping at each pile where the hay would be pitch forked up onto the cart.

It was my job to stay on the cart and as the hay was forked up the pitchfork would be turned over so that the sharp prongs faced down. I would then throw myself onto the forkful until the fork was withdrawn and then arrange the hay on the bed of the cart between the 'Lades'. These lades were a wooden framework erected at the front and rear of the cart to enable the hay to be piled high on the cart without slipping off when the cart moved.

When the load was as high as the lades

and I could pile no more on, neither could the pitchers fork any higher, we would set off across the field and into the paddock, with me balanced on top of the load.

I loved this part of the proceedings. When we arrived at the Dutch barn in the paddock, which was a roof of corrugated iron supported on high wooden poles, with two side walls also of corrugated iron, I commenced to throw down the hay to the others who had walked up from the field. Using their pitchforks they started to form the Rick in the Dutch barn, the sides sloping in very gently to form a perfect stack.

As the height of the stack increased and reached the level of the hay in the cart, I would move to the stack and help build it carrying armfuls of hay around, whilst the stronger ones stood on the cart and pitch forked it up. So it went on, load after load, until the field was clear and the stack built. I would then slide down one of the barn uprights and we all repaired to the farm kitchen for a large harvest supper.

Were we ever glad that the job was over and the winter fodder was safely in, to say nothing of the fact that we could take it relatively easy on the morrow.

The only difference between the end of

our operation and that of the larger farms was that they would sometimes use the Huxtable Rake to form the finished hay into rows, and then employ a large horse drawn rake made of horizontal tines sliding on the ground, guided by a man holding two big handles behind.

With this they would 'sweep' the hay to a corner of the field to build a stack. As the sweep arrived at the stack the operator would have to lift the handles and let the tines reverse to dump the load of hay.

After the stack was built in an open field it would then have to be thatched, normally with straw but if there was none available, with tightly packed bundles of hay, lined up to deflect the rain water off the stack. The thatching was held in place by Hazel sticks that had been split lengthwise into four pieces.

Each piece was then twisted, whilst still green, and folded in the middle into a 'U'. The ends were then sharpened and the resulting staves driven through the thatching into the stack. By the time the stack was used these staves had dried and hardened and broke easily at the twist forming the perfect basis for making into swords for us boys!

After the hay harvest we would visit the

stack on frequent occasions and stick an iron bar into it. When we withdrew it we would feel the end to gauge the temperature of the stack. In this way we hoped to avert a fire breaking out in the stack. Normally stacks burst into flame at the same time as Barnstaple Fair and it was generally thought that if your stack lasted until after the Fair you were safe.

The stack would settle and compress the hay into a solid block. The only way to extract portions for feeding to the animals was to cut sections with a hay knife. This was a blade about three feet long with a large two handed handle on the top and was not easy to manipulate.

Drum mowers, Haybobs, Balers and Flat eight systems or Round Balers really took the work out of haymaking when they arrived.

Even more now has silage making supplanted haymaking due in no small part to the vagaries of the Devon weather, but nothing can replace the smell of new mown hay. There is also nothing like the smell of a handful of well made hay in the depths of winter to bring back the thought of summer.

I well remember, as my first experience of silage, a cart full of it passed us in Station Road. I asked Laurie what the foul smelling load was. He said something that I heard as 'Hen Sledge', which I interpreted as Chicken Manure, which to my mind certainly explained the aroma.

In later years when I made my own hay I still revelled in the lovely smell, and the satisfaction of trials and tribulations overcome, when feeding it to my sheep and cattle in midwinter.

Chapter 8

Bratton School
Infants Class

So it was after my fifth birthday in the autumn of 1940 that I recommenced my education, at Bratton Fleming School. It was not then, as now, called a Primary school as it was the only school most pupils ever attended.

Bratton School today

The school leaving age was fourteen and children attended this school from the age of five until they left, to work mainly on the farms.

Very few ever had ambitions towards employment in Barnstaple, and the local farms, being very small both in size and income, needed the free labour of all the family to survive, and indeed they operated at just survival level.

No luxuries were ever seen on these farms, no plumbing, water was from wells, stream, or occasionally, to the high farmhouses, from the water rams. Electricity had not reached the countryside still, and was not to do so until the end of the 1940s. There were very few radios in the village and none on the farms.

Newspapers were not delivered with the milk at that time as happened later, for the whole village obtained its milk from local farmers who sent their daughters around with a large can from door to door, in our area Vera Heal performed this task. She would walk through the village with pails of milk and a dipper with which she would fill peoples lidded milk cans which they hung on their gates.

Farming families were therefore totally self sufficient, raising all their own food and buying little more than salt. They baked their own bread from their own flour ground at one of the two village mills, milk from their own cows and meat from their own animals and vegetables from the garden.

Clothes were a great expense and were therefore purchased to last. Hobnail boots and corduroy trousers for all the males of all ages, (except the farmers and farm workers who wore breeches and leggings), and very patched hand me down ill fitting shirts.

I arrived at school on my first day in the same garb as the rest as I was by now an established resident. Hobnail boots with long leather laces tied in 'chains', grey stockings, corduroy shorts and grey shirt, in my case being unusual in that it fitted and was not yet patched.

One other boy started the same day as me, Raymond Bennett, as he was rather plump he was immediately nicknamed Buster and was never known by any other name from then on by adults or children.

Having been handed over by our parents to the tender mercies of the Headmistress, one 'Granny' Noble, we were escorted into the infants classroom where the five, six and seven year olds were taught, and sat in little wooden armchairs in front of the class to be introduced to the other pupils.

All the classroom windows were very high up in the walls so looking out of them would not distract us. Heating in all the rooms was by a coke stove, which only warmed you if you were right on top of it.

The London Blitz had not yet got underway so the class still consisted of local children. The school having only two rooms and a lobby, the larger room was split by a folding partition. One half contained the eight to ten year olds whilst the other the eleven to thirteen.

This top class was very rarely up to complement as the pupils had to stand in on the farms for any sick elders, either acting as cook and mother in the case of the girls, or running the farm in the case of the boys.

Also at busy times such as lambing, haymaking, corn harvest etc. the children were needed at home and were kept there, to the despair of the teachers. The fourteen year old graduates therefore were normally adept at simple mathematics, as they used that in their farm work, but reading and writing were not normally very great accomplishments.

Buster and I were regarded with some curiosity by our classmates, both male and female, most of whom we had never seen before. Bratton school not only served all the outlying farms in the area, covering a distance that even my ramblings had not yet taken me, but also some other villages like Stoke Rivers, from where children were bussed each day in an ancient station wagon by Archie Crook. Those from hamlets like Stowford were collected by a taxi from the Lower Shop, also referred to as 'Norman and Woolacotts'.

Some children had to walk in from the eastern side up to three miles each day across country and along muddy cart tracks, but those on the northern and southern sides, if on the transports route, had the benefit of arriving in style. These included Peter and Kathleen Shapland, Charlie Prouse and Vera Ridd-Jones, among others.

Many pupils, on rainy days, arrived with their boots and stockings plastered in thick mud and their shirts and shorts soaked, despite the hessian corn sacks that they used to cover their heads and shoulders. There was no such thing as an anorak and raincoats or oilskins were well beyond most of their means.

There were a few other pupils that Buster and I had seen previously but did not really know, also some that we did. Raymond and Gordon Lott, and Derek Marshall who formed the 'Bottom of the Village' gang, and Pat Parkhouse who with us and Laurie Tribe would form the 'Middle of the Village' gang, destined to become notorious for miles around in the next few years. Laurie being a year junior to us was not presently at school.

Our two gangs would have intermittent truces during such times as Bratton Fair, or at corn harvest when our combined strength would sometimes be required in the pursuit of rabbits but in the main we were rivals and kept our distance, especially as the Bottom Gang was a year or two older than us and tended to whip any of us caught alone.

Having been introduced to the other boys and girls we were issued with our slates and slate pencils, these we were to use for the next three years, writing paper being too scarce to allow infants to use, and ink being too dangerous. We were allowed chalk to draw on the blackboards that surrounded the classroom. We had small sea shells to help us in counting and arithmetic.

Lessons proved initially very easy for me, copying letters from the blackboard was simple after the writing I had been doing in Thornton Heath at the age of two. Arithmetic consisted of counting sea shells which we were given and had to set in patterns according to the required numbers.

The ease with which I mastered this soon led me into trouble as I became disenchanted with the lessons and did not bother to try. My expertise at writing soon disappeared and I drifted behind the rest of the class, especially the girls who were exceptionally neat.

My arithmetic also suffered. We were rewarded for work with a star system, used I am sure by primary teachers today. Good work was rewarded by half a red star and exceptional work by a full red star. Poor work received a half a black star, whilst very bad work warranted a full black star.

Within a year of us commencing school Granny Noble was replaced by a Headmaster, one Sam Bentham who was to remain at the school until the late Seventies. Granny used to punish malefactors by slapping them on the arms very hard with her hand. Sam however brought with him a proper, four foot long, thin cane.

Sam instituted an inspection of work and decreed that any pupil who had received black half stars during the week would receive as many strokes of the cane. On Friday afternoons we in the infants had play afternoons when we were allowed to bring one toy to school or alternatively choose a toy from the classroom toy box, kept in a cupboard.

This toy box was full of treasures, the best being a wooden Noah's Ark complete with all the animals. Friday afternoons were looked forward to with immense pleasure therefore by all, except yours truly, and any other with black stars, as it was then that Sam used to carry out his inspections.

My name always appeared on the board where the red and black stars were displayed, and never accompanied by a red one. I used to play with my allotted toy, or play chasing each other under the desks, whilst keeping one eye fearfully on the door, hoping that this day something would happen to stop Sam coming to the classroom but it never did.

About halfway through the afternoon the door would open and in he would come, cane hanging over his right arm, and his words never varied. "Good afternoon children, David Beckett go into the lobby, and who else have we today."

I cannot remember a single Friday during my time in the infants when I was not in perpetual fear of Sam's cane. Mark you, I was caned on other days as well but that was for other misdemeanours.

I would say, however, that those canings, whilst doing me no psychological harm that I am aware of, also did me no good in the way of improving my educational talents, caning is definitely not a cure for laziness.

I was not keen on school and as I had a pony I sometimes left the paddock gate open when I went. The pony would follow me to school, and into the playground, Sam would come into class and tell me to take it back home which always took me a very long time. We used to call skipping school 'Mitching', I wonder where the term originates.

As it was wartime we all had gas masks in cardboard cartons suspended from a string around our necks. We only took these to school on days when we had exercises, then we had to practise putting them on. Some of the very small children had ones that looked like elephants, pink with trunks.

We were also given half a pint of milk a day to supplement our diet. This came in a glass bottle with a cardboard lid with a small press out hole in the middle through which we inserted a straw.

Our lessons in this class were punctuated on several occasions by the sound of enormous explosions that rattled the windows and made us all jump. They were the results of practising bridge blowing by the Royal Engineers and Commandoes who blew up all the old Barnstaple to Lynton Railway bridges.

Luckily they confined themselves to the ones where the track crossed the deep lanes and left the ones where the roads or lanes crossed the tracks.

Towards the end of 1940 the village started to receive it's quota of evacuees from the cities. This influx of pupils meant that the school buildings were inadequate so the Village Hall was utilised, this could be divided into two rooms by a wooden partition and the infant classes were moved there.

Teachers for a time were in short supply and therefore the older pupils were given the job of teaching the infants. Imagine my embarrassment when Beryl appeared in our classroom to teach us.

I was pretty uncontrollable at the best of times but there was no way that she could control a class with me in it, and no threats worked, even her regular complaints to Mother and Mother's remonstrances to me did not work for long and my poor sister dreaded those days she had to take my class.

We had a high turnover of teachers at this time as they arrived from the cities and in many cases returned there quite quickly. I remember we had a Miss Broom and a Miss Coles and I always wondered whether we would get a Miss Scuttle or Miss Shovel.

Playtimes were in the lower playground for the infants, we had several standard games varying, in common with other children nationally, as the seasons.

I still do not understand, although I have heard it said by many people from different parts of the country, why a game can be all the rage one day and a few days later no-one will be playing it. We played hopscotch, statues, which consisted of leaping off a hedge on command and remaining stationary in any position you landed, tag or tick, among others.

We also wore these hobnail boots and one of us would 'rookie' down whilst two others towed him the length of the playground to see if he could generate sparks and to see how hot the hobnails got. We would then feel his hobnails to see who got the hottest, Buster normally won that but it was not until many years later, as an engineer, that I fathomed out that this was due to the extra friction caused by his weight.

These boots were quite a fashion item. Initially we had round hobnails with tips and cues. Later we changed to a sort of 'ace of clubs' pattern stud and you were naff (a term not invented then but very applicable), if you had round studs. Similarly we first had our long leather laces wound around each other to produce a long rat's tail, but later plaited them into chains. You had to have the right look.

When we went outside for PE we took oval raffia mats to lie on and for team games we had different coloured bands which we wore over one shoulder. They tried at one time to teach us country dancing. We also played one game of looping in and out of a ring of children holding hands singing, 'The big ship sails through the Alley Alley O", I cannot remember the purpose of this, if there was one.

For decisions we either 'Dipped', 'One potato, two potato', 'Up the pole down the pole monkey chew tobacco', and sometimes one which is definitely not Politically Correct nowadays so I will not mention it here, or we spat on one side of a stone and tossed it, calling 'wet or dry'. When pursued to exhaustion we would cross our fingers and cry 'fains', I have since heard that this expression is used all over England with different pronunciations. I wonder the origin of it.

When necessary to be excused we would put our hand up and ask 'Please Miss may I go up top'. I see recently that it is government policy that all schools should have inside toilets.

I see little advantage in that as, if it was pouring with rain, our requests were much less frequent as we had to trek to the top of the upper playground. The only other thing I remember about the toilets was we would have competitions, to see who could pee the highest up the wall of the urinal.

I think I caught most things going at the school, chickenpox, measles etc. I fell down in the playground and cut my knee, a teacher washed it with a filthy rag in the unhygienic washbasins in the lobby that resulted in a nice case of impetigo.

I caught fleas, as there was no such thing as Suleo shampoo then, my mother bought a scurf comb and used to comb my hair over a newspaper every night cracking the fleas between her nails until I was cured.

We had visits from the nit nurse, Nurse Edwards, who normally found her time not wasted. I remember Pat being very proud of his fair locks, and not wishing to have them rummaged through by the nurse, going home at lunchtime and smothering his hair with brylcreem.

It worked, as when it came to his turn she paused with her fingers over the sticky mass and said, "I think you are OK! Next". Many boys got ringworm, which we four escaped, but they would come to school with their heads shaved and purple with Gentian Violet, the only remedy in those days.

When we reached the top of the infants class Sam instituted a new torture for the senior infants. He took his seat at the Mistress's desk in the middle classroom when that class was engaged in PT and called us all out of our class, one by one, to stand in front of him. We then had to recite our tables both forwards and backwards from our twice times table progressing twice weekly to our twelve times table.

This was a terrible ordeal for us as merely standing in front of Sam took away the power of speech. Years later though, when I was Head of a Maths Department at an RAF apprentice school, I wished my pupils had learned their tables in the same way.

It is hard teaching Differential Calculus to students who need calculators to multiply six by eight. It is also frustrating to buy three pairs of socks at £1.20 each to have the assistant reach for his calculator to work out the bill.

Every morning we all assembled in the top classroom for prayers and a hymn. After this, sometimes we had choral singing to the accompaniment of the piano. We would be arranged in lines, tallest at the back, shortest at the front, and under Sam's stern eye have to sing loudly. The only song I can remember apart from the Christmas Carols is, 'The Ash Grove'.

Whilst we were at play, about once a week an old man, Basil Fanshawe who lived at Hollywell, further down Station Road past the school, used to walk past. He would always look in at the playground gate and search his pockets for pennies which he would then throw in the air over us and we would scramble to get. You could buy so much with a penny, a lovely hot bun fresh baked from Granny Ewens shop, a whole packet of saccharine, an Oxo cube, or a box of matches, always useful for lighting our many fires.

This continued for several years until we heard that old Basil had died, we were very sad as we really appreciated his generosity, and I well remember us boys standing outside the church gate opposite the school watching the stone mason carving a memorial to Basil in the gatepost.

Our appreciation however had not stopped us whilst he was alive from scrumping the apples from his orchard, nor did his death interrupt this pleasurable pastime, even though the grounds of Holywell were patrolled by Alfie Lavercombe with a shotgun.

My father was not particularly impressed with Basil's money tossing being the only treat for the school children and so he got a group of parents together to organise an annual Christmas party for the school. At the first one in 1940 he arranged for a Punch and Judy show, also a conjuror, which we all enjoyed very much.

In later years the party consisted of a games session followed by an enormous feast, although rationing was in full swing. In the country the food was produced and the locals therefore ate well, and gave generously.

The tables groaned under a load of home baked goodies, homemade jams and clotted cream, but amazingly the item in greatest demand was plain bread and farmhouse butter.

Why this should be so I do not know but it is still true to this day. The tradition of the party still exists and should do so for ever as in his declining years my father set up a Charitable Trust for the school to provide the means to finance the party for all time.

After the tea, a cinematograph projector was supplied by Darks of Barnstaple and cartoon films were shown, this was the only time many children ever saw a film, and they were looked forward to and talked about all year.

Before going home each child was presented with a National Savings book containing a sixpenny savings stamp, paid for by Father, later increased to one shilling, and in more recent years replaced by the outright gift of ten pence.

In 1986 after my fathers death, the then Headmistress Miss Passmore decided that, in view of the now commonplace TV the film show should be dispensed with, which was not a popular move with the children, as some parents informed me. Apart from that change the party still persists, I understand, in its original form.

It was attended every year by both my mother and father until their deaths, and after that I always made the effort to attend until I moved out of the area, and passed over Trusteeship of the 'Beckett Trust' to the then headmistress.

Chapter 9

Traps and Snares

I would advise anyone born in the last three decades, or of a squeamish nature, to skip this chapter. The 1940s was an era in the twentieth century when ideas, morals, and way of life were totally different from acceptable practices in the twenty-first century. I have to include these descriptions if I am accurately to portray country life of those times. One must remember that country folk even today have a different outlook and standards with respect to wildlife than those reared in a city.

In those days of subsistence farming all means possible were taken to protect crops and farm animals from predators. Farmers and farm workers needed every scrap of meat obtainable to maintain their strength for hard manual labour as they did not have the benefits of today's mechanical help.

People in the cities too, under strict rationing, were only too happy to supplement their diet with rabbit and pigeon meat etc. without a thought as to how it had been obtained in the countryside. Shooting was probably the most humane method but cartridges were hard to come by in wartime and would not have provided the quantity of meat required to supplement the nation's rations. Many of the practices I describe are illegal today but were the accepted norm in those days.

Mr Mitchell left our employ, as did his daughter Stella who in the early days was our 'Daily'. He was replaced by Bill Bale on the understanding that he could keep one cow at Craigside providing he looked after ours. I do seem to remember he played favourites at feeding times and his milking pail always seemed fuller than ours.

However he taught me a lot about country life. He had the rabbiting concession for Dullam's farm at The Barton by Bratton Cross amongst others, and would take me with him in the mornings. I would help carry the traps and rabbits. I was quite happy to go with him after milking in the early hours, although it was a long walk for my little legs.

We would start by collecting sacks to carry the rabbits, and a bucket, hammer and builders trowel from a barn at the farm. He would sieve a bucket full of earth, dug up with the trowel and we would proceed out along the steep cleave. There were literally hundreds if not thousands of rabbit holes among the bracken covered slopes and in the ancient hedge banks.

Bill would normally have set about one hundred gin traps previously. These traps are illegal today, but consisted of two steel jaws, teethed, and held closed by a strong spring handle, to the end of the handle was attached a length of steel chain, on the other end of which was a steel spike about one foot long.

The trap was set by compressing the spring handle with your foot, opening the jaws to lie flat, raising the flat tiller plate to the horizontal and securing it in place with a catch. Any pressure on the plate would depress it causing the release of the catch and the jaws would snap shut.

The whole trap was secured to the ground by the spike which was driven in full length with the hammer. All types of trap were never cleaned and always rust coated as the animals have a keen sense of smell so you handled the traps as little as possible.

In order to catch a rabbit you looked for a hole that showed recent signs of occupancy, fresh earth outside, fresh droppings or paw prints. Then, just at the entrance to the burrow you scraped a hole with the trowel to accommodate the set jaws of the trap. You kept your hands away from the earth otherwise the rabbit would smell you.

Having placed the trap in this depression you banged the spike into the ground to hold it firmly and then, again with the trowel, sprinkled the sieved earth from the bucket over the tiller of the trap concealing it completely. The trap would then be left in place until the following morning.

We would set off along the cleave, inspecting all the traps and retrieving the trapped rabbits. They were normally already dead, whether from shock or blood loss I do not know as they usually were only caught by one leg.

We would retrieve them and, if it was a first catch, reset the trap at the same burrow. If we had caught several rabbits there or if we had not caught one for two nights we would move the trap to a fresh burrow. Sometimes a fox would have been caught in the trap in which case we never saw the fox as it would have bitten off its leg at the break and only its paw would remain in the trap.

Having completed the round of the hundred traps we would have about fifty or sixty rabbits and would sit down to paunch them, i.e. clean them ready for market. Having carried them home to Bill's house they would be collected daily by a Barnstaple butcher, such as Mr Percy Brend, who would despatch them to London or Bristol by train.

They were transported in wooden crates like today's milk bottle plastic crates. This was the prime source of income for the trappers and a lifeline for the needy folks in the cities.

It was on this farm later in the war that I remember a German, or was it Italian, prisoner of war was employed. We boys used to go down and talk to him, sitting on a fallen tree. He made ships in bottles which he sold, I think for ten shillings (50p). My father would not let me buy one but I believe the rest did. I wonder if anyone has still got one.

Whilst Bill took all the trapped rabbits for himself he instructed me in the art of setting snares and I was allowed to set a dozen snares on the cleave. This was a far more difficult form of capture. The snare consisted of a running noose of woven brass wire secured at the end with two long brown strings.

You had to cut a stick from the hedge and tie the string to it securely. You then had to carefully search the bracken or long grass for a rabbit run. They normally followed the same path so the runs were well worn but sometimes a new run would show up as a trail in the early morning dew on the grass.

You found a place where the grass or bracken beside the run was thick enough to hide the snare, its prop and securing stick. Opening the noose enough to freely admit the rabbits head it would be held off the ground at the right height by using a twig with a split in the top to support the wire adjacent to the noose.

The whole was then anchored firmly to the ground by driving the stick well in. The expertise came from not only choosing a good run but also in the size and height off the ground of the noose and the quality of the concealment.

If I was fortunate, especially with my inexpertise, I would catch one or two rabbits a night in my twelve snares. Bill would buy these from me at a discount or I would take them home to my mother very proudly, for lunch. I would paunch them myself, we boys always carried pocket knives as a matter of course for the hundreds of uses we put them to.

They had to have the words 'Real Lamb Foot' engraved on the blade if you were not to lose face. As I farmed for some years after leaving the RAF I had to acquire one again for all the farm tasks, and as I write this I still have one identical in my pocket as a matter of habit, although it comes in useful for much more mundane tasks these days.

I think it was Pat who instructed me in the setting of mole traps as he used to till them in the Cricket field. These consisted of two vertical sprung handles which, when compressed, opened four jaws which were propped open by a circular ring tiller.

The idea was that the mole would come along the run popping his head though the ring and spring the trap. The sprung jaws were so strong that the mole was instantly crushed and did not suffer. I have never seen a live one taken out of one of these traps.

To set them, we examined the ground either side of a fresh mole hill to ascertain the slight raising of the turf which indicated the direction of the run.

Carefully digging down with the pen knife we would make a rectangular opening in the run just big enough to accommodate the jaws of the trap. Inserting the trap we then sealed the hole around it with clats of earth to exclude all light from the run. When re-entering the field next day you could see if the trap had been sprung by the state of the spring handles, if they were still closed you would leave the trap alone for another try.

It was Derek Marshall, one day, in a kind mood, who showed me how to skin moles and pin the skins out on a board to dry in the sun after they had been rubbed with salt. The cured skins would then be taken in to the glove factory in Barnstaple where they paid up to sixpence a skin, (about 2p in today's money). This augmented the boys' pocket money, if they got any pocket money, and did the farmers a service by ridding their fields of the pest.

Chapter 10

Ferrets and Fish

Members of this generation may rejoin me now as the practices I am about to describe are still carried on in the country but I would advise the squeamish and city dwellers to pass on to the next chapter.

Bill Bale, like many others kept ferrets. These were not used for the current practice of inserting into trouser legs as pet ferrets are today. They were wild ferrets and kept bloodthirsty by being fed mainly on rabbits' innards and milk.

Bill taught me how to handle ferrets, holding them just behind their heads. He also taught me how to make a 'Cope' out of string. This was like a muzzle consisting of a small loop of string that kept the ferrets mouth tightly closed secured to a larger loop that went around the head behind the ears to hold the first in place. Thus muzzled the ferret could neither bite its owner nor attack a rabbit.

Ferreting took two forms, one was netting. You found a Devon bank that had numerous rabbit holes and staked nets over all holes bar one. Into this hole you introduced the coped ferret and it immediately disappeared in search of its prey. Being unable to attack the rabbits it merely chased them out into the nets where they were quickly retrieved and dispatched by 'necking'.

The other method was to dispense with the nets and station one man with a shotgun on either side of the hedge to shoot the rabbits as they emerged from their holes. This could be a little more dangerous as occasionally a rabbit would pop out of a hole on top of the hedge.

You had to have faith in the other gunslinger then, in that he would not shoot across the top of the hedge just where you were standing. I did hear of one nasty wounding which occurred this way, I believe in Haxton lane, but I am not sure of the participants.

Sometimes the ferret would give up on his work and go to sleep if it could not find any rabbits. Then we would stake out some innards at the entrance to the burrow to encourage it to emerge. However, occasionally it would slip its cope and kill a rabbit underground and start to feast.

In this case the only recourse was to send a line ferret down, that is one with a long piece of string attached to it that would find the first in order to join in the feast. By the length of the line run out and from experience (not always correct), we would judge where in the bank the ferret was laid up and with pick and shovel attempt to dig it out. This was a long arduous task and normally meant the end of ferreting for that day.

One day my uncle Arch, a cobbler by trade, was staying at Craigside on a visit from Horley. He only had one leg and I was always agog to see his primitive cork false one and the way it was secured. He expressed a desire to do some shooting so Father lent him his shotgun and suggested I borrowed a ferret from Bill Bale. This I duly did and to his credit Bill let me have his favourite which I duly coped and carried home.

Uncle and I walked, or rather he proceeded like Hop-along-Cassidy, to the bottom of Craigside field. It was not good hunting ground as there were not many rabbits, for our livestock kept the grass very short. There was also no corn grown by any neighbouring farmers to attract the rabbits to the vicinity. Many of the few burrows were old and looked deserted but I found a likely one and popped the ferret down and retreated to stand behind uncle with his loaded and cocked gun.

Yes, you are probably ahead of me, out of another burrow popped the ferrets head and off went the gun. Down went my uncle with the recoil but unfortunately his aim had been true and as he lay there he heard me in a pitiful voice say "You've shot Bill's best ferret".

Bill was not amused when I took the body back to him and explained what had happened but I believe uncle reimbursed him quite handsomely. Uncle did no more shooting on that or subsequent visits though.

On Boxing Day some of the villagers either hunted or followed the hounds. The rest of the village sportsmen had an open invitation to go ferreting on Whitefield Down, between Friendship and Challacombe. When Rex was home for Christmas I always went along with my elders. We would spend an energetic day walking over the frozen Downs, with a packed lunch. There were literally thousands of rabbit warrens there.

Another pastime I enjoyed, albeit a solitary one and illegal in that it was poaching, was fishing. Now my brother, Rex, used to enjoy fishing and did so until he died, often visiting Dulverton for that purpose later in life.

However he did it the conventional way and I used to accompany him with his rod down to Button river where he would stand for hours, and I would get totally bored, with him muttering "Be quiet" every time I opened my mouth. It was very rare that he would catch a trout.

My method, and I cannot remember who suggested it to me, was far more efficient. I obtained some line, gut and fishhooks from my brother's creel and dug a tin of worms from the garden. Thus equipped I would set off about dusk over the stile at the bottom of Craigside field, down Farmer Vickery's two fields and over the stile into the lane. Just inside the lane on the right I would pass the entrance to a path through Fanshawes' wood.

Just inside the entrance was a clump of bamboo which we boys used to steal for bow and spear making. Opposite this clump was a privet bush clipped into the shape of a settee. There was much interesting topiary in their grounds, whether the result of Alfie Lavercombe's work or another gardener I do not know.

Next I would pass the blown up railway bridge and the public footpath beyond it to Bratton station. On, down the deep lane, until

Bratton Mill came in sight. Then it was over the hedge and creep down to the water. I usually set my first line near the footbridge that carried the public footpath over the river.

A stretch for night lines

Why I chose my first line so close to habitation I am not sure, it may have been bravado or that just below the wooden bridge the river widened out into shallows that were easier to wade. I'd tie the ends of the line to a tree on either bank concealing it in the grass and allowing it to loop slightly under water.

Securing four hooks baited with worms along the line with lengths of catgut, I would proceed a few hundred yards upstream and repeat the process, in another shallow stretch, and then return home.

Very early next morning just as the sun was getting up and the dew on the grass wet my boots, I would return to the scene of the crime, normally seeing at least one silvery gleam on each line. I'd retrieve two or three beautiful trout, gleaming silver with red spots, they were magnificent. Collecting both lines I'd return home and present the fish to Mother who would cook them for breakfast. From river to plate within the hour, that is the way to taste trout.

The other area we boys tried to fish was Lancybrook, below the mill. George, Laurie's brother, was adept at tickling them under the bank, and tried to teach us. I do not think any of us had much success although we tried for hours lying on our stomachs. I certainly never managed to catch one by this method. We also later tried shooting them with air rifles but found the water slowed the pellets down too much. We did learn a lot about air to water refraction in doing this though.

Chapter 11

Bird's Nesting

Nowadays this hobby is completely illegal with heavy fines or even prison sentences being imposed upon egg collectors, but then it was the norm for every village boy to have an egg collection. Before their natural habitats were destroyed by modern agricultural methods there were far more wild birds of all species. I am sure that the eggs we collected did minimal harm to the numbers and were much fewer than those taken by other predators.

The number of eggs we would allow ourselves to take depended on the species, and the finder of the nest would get first choice, unless he already had an egg of the type in his collection. We would always carry a pin in our lapel for the purpose of making a very small hole in each end of the egg and blowing the contents out. Sometimes the egg would be addled and broke during this operation and we would get covered with a stinking mess.

We would never take more than one egg from a Robin or a Wren, the various types of thrushes or blackbirds. However, when it came to Magpies, Rooks and Crows we would take what we needed and destroy the rest, and possibly the nest as well. Anyone who has seen the injuries these birds can cause to new born lambs, or old ewes who are stuck on their backs, will understand our motives in this respect.

Sparrow Hawks', Kestrels' and especially Buzzards' eggs were highly prized and quite rarely did we find one of their nests. We thought these were such beautiful birds that we never took more than one egg from them although they were also destructive, carrion eating birds.

We would carefully carry our spoils home and label them and place them in a cotton wool box. I had an Egg Collectors handbook which showed pictures of the birds, their eggs and nests, so we would be able to identify them.

This pastime taught us a lot about nature and the bird's habitat, some build the most beautiful and cunningly constructed nests. I would encourage anyone to take up bird's nesting, not to rob the nests these days as we did, but armed with a digital camera for recording their habitat.

There were places, now long gone mostly, where we could be certain of finding the nests of certain species. We knew most of the trees where we could find crow's or rook's nests and we also knew where to find many other species.

Rook's nests were particularly hard to access. They always build in colonies and choose a group of the highest trees in the vicinity, invariably difficult to climb. We never did climb those at the entrance to Rectory Drive.

The unclimbed trees

In a triangular wood near Button a Kestrel used to nest, in Bulls Linhay was a Barn Owl. In a barn down Loxhore lane past the river were always pigeons, whilst under Tidicombe Cleave was not only a Buzzard but also a Heron.

We never got a Heron's egg as we always found the nest empty but we saw the Heron several times. It was a massive nest at the very top of the tallest tree in the area, so tall in fact that we were all frightened to climb up to it although, with the exception of Buster, we were all expert climbers.

We eventually drew lots, I think, or 'Dipped' and I lost. It was the most frightening climb I ever made and all to no avail as the nest was empty but it was big enough for me to sit in and rest before the equally perilous descent.

One thing always puzzled us. At dusk we would congregate outside Harold Parkin's window. If we stood out in the road and threw small pebbles in the air numerous bats would dive on them. They would confuse the sonic echoes on the pebbles with a flying insect. We never found out where the bats roosted during the day. We certainly never saw any on our excursions up the church tower, which would have been the most obvious place.

Chapter 12

Bicycles

Christmas morning 1941 I came downstairs to find at the bottom the hearts desire of a five year old boy, a bicycle. My old tricycle which had come down from Croydon had never recovered from Laurie's brother hitching a ride down the road standing on the back axle. Father had tried to get it repaired in County garage but it was never the same. Whereas the axle took the weight of the others, even Buster, George being older and much heavier sadly broke it.

This bicycle was brand new and bright blue. No self respecting boy would be seen dead on it these days as it was known as a 'Fairy Cycle', but the term was not used in that way then. I, misunderstanding the phrase that Tommy Handly used, on the radio in ITMA when a word was censored, called it after what I thought I heard him call his, which he always referred to as his "Blue Pencil bicycle".

I was overwhelmed, and remember sitting in the saddle immediately, holding on to the door frame, and moving forwards and back. I could not wait to get out on it and after breakfast persuaded Rex to come into the drive with me and show me how to ride. He ran up and down the drive a few times holding on to the back of the saddle and then said, as he was puffed that we would have a break and then go into the paddock where there was more room. By this time I had got the hang of steering it but was not prepared for his little ploy.

He held the saddle while I mounted at the top of the paddock and shouted 'Off we go', so off I pedalled. I was half way down before I realised that not only was I going faster than of late but I was also unaccompanied. I had mastered the steering but not the brakes, so came to an abrupt stop in the hedge and made a very close acquaintance with the crab apple tree. I think my tears were short lived in the excitement. I suspect this is how most children are taught to ride. So I was then on my own.

I believe the other three learnt on that bike in short order, even Buster, although he took a few more falls than most, but for some time it was the only bike between the four of us. This caused a few problems. You cannot progress very well when one is riding and three are walking. You do not want to push a bike when you can ride so we soon developed our own circus act. Because of our difference in size the various positions required quickly became apparent.

I, being middle sized as well as being the owner, took the saddle. Laurie being the smallest could squeeze in front of me on the crossbar. Buster being the largest sat on the handlebars facing forward and Pat being the tallest stood on the back forks.

This did mean that, as I was the only motive force, we could progress along the flat reasonably well but uphill was a no no. However going down hill was a piece of cake and we used to whiz down Bratton hill with gusto. Mounting the bike by the four of us had its moments, but dismounting had variations. At the first sign of danger Pat just stepped off and was on his own, Laurie normally made a flying leap sideways knocking my hand off the handlebars.

Buster was in the forefront of any contact with a hedge, and cushioned the bike and myself from harm. This was a bit hard on Buster at times but we felt he was well padded to absorb the shock and he never came to serious harm.

This was not quite as dangerous a pastime then, as it would be today, for there were only three or four cars in the village. My father's, who was in Barum all day, Norman and Woolacott's rarely used taxi, Nurse Moor's and Mr Lewis' at Benton. There were plenty of horse and carts on the road but these were slow and easily avoided.

We toured Bratton like this for a considerable time until one day we rounded the corner by the White Hart, coming down Bratton hill at a fair rate of knots, to find Fred Bale in the middle of the road. We managed to miss him but he turned a few shades paler as he flung himself out of our way. In my defence I would say that forward vision was somewhat impaired by Buster and Laurie, and Buster on the handlebars also did little to improve my steering capabilities.

Anyway Fred was off to my parents in quick time to inform them that not only were we a danger to ourselves, about which he cared little, not being the most popular of his acquaintances, but also to others. He said that he felt we would do someone great harm, himself not excepted, if we were allowed to continue.

Thus it was that, when I could not find my bike one morning, my Father told me that, as I had been stupid enough to leave it out the night before, some tramp must have stolen it.

All of us were disconsolate over this

but, despite our inquiries of all and sundry, could get no further information regarding its fate. Some weeks later we were playing on the top of the haystack in the Dutch barn at Craigside when someone pushed Pat over backwards. He cried out in pain and, rubbing his back, said he must have hit it on the handle of the hay knife.

On investigation it proved not to be the knife but the handlebars of my bike. We immediately realised what had happened and joyously lowered it from the stack and were out on the road again.

When Father came home I told him it was not stolen after all but hidden by some prankster. He could not admit he had lied to me and as I never left it out again he was stymied. I probably did get a lecture on road safety but as I cannot remember it, it obviously left little impression.

Soon after this however each of the others received their own cycles. Whether this was the result of a meeting of parents who wanted to see their children reach maturity, we shall never know. This did not improve the safety of walking in Bratton with no pavements, as now the locals had to deal with us coming down the hill four abreast taking up the whole road and playing chicken, with no brakes.

The other rather sad consequence of the cycles was that I forsook my pony which got fat in the field from lack of exercise. How could I leave my friends to ride bikes whilst I rode solitary on horseback? I remember my last ride was to Loxhore to get the pony shod.

Jim Lavercombe had retired from the Smithy and the nearest alternative was at Loxhore. Father walked all the way there and back with me, for company, and afterwards took the pony away to sell. I was very hardhearted at the time and was only glad to be free of the nagging I was receiving about exercising it.

As all young boys, we put our cycles through much misuse. We constructed tracks over the humps in a field down Station road, and more tracks at the entrance to Rectory Drive by Lower Shop. We never aspired to 'wheelies' like today's youth and I do not know if the bikes were capable of it in those days. I do remember on a few occasions daring each other to disconnect the brakes and attempt Bratton Hill, such idiots we were.

It was in this state one day that I rounded the corner by Lower Shop, going at top speed, to find that outside Rachel Champion's house the road was completely blocked by two cattle transporters, the drivers of which were having a chat.

I tried unsuccessfully to turn into Haxton lane but my speed was too great and I came off, sliding on my side, ruining my shirt and shorts to say nothing of my arm and leg on the gravel, whilst the bike crashed into the milk churns at the entrance to the lane.

Pat's father was the expert at mending punctures. When we tried ourselves we usually found that, after a struggle getting the tyre off with spoon handles, messing with patches, rubber solution and French chalk, the so say repaired result would have extra punctures having been pinched on tyre removal or replacement.

We also had problems with cone adjustments on the axles and the repair of overworked Sturmey Archer three speed hubs was a nightmare. Not for us today's twenty gear derailler gears.

We would put old cigarette packets on the back brake brackets to rub against the spokes so we sounded like motor bikes. This added a noise nuisance to our other failings. I suppose at least people could hear us coming and leap for the safety of the hedge.

Chapter 13

Corn Harvest

As in earlier chapters, this one contains items that the squeamish might not wish to read. I can only reiterate that these were different times with, by necessity, different moral codes. Country folk always have and always will see things differently to townsfolk. Animals, whether domestic or wild, are not reared to be pets but for food or producers of food.

I have never known a cruel farmer yet, or one who has not cared about or grown attached to some of his livestock. He is in business though, and has still to send them off to slaughter when the time is ripe. One once said to me "Where you have livestock you also have deadstock and the only thing to love on the farm is your wife". Hard but true, so read on bearing all this in mind.

How it happened we never knew, it could be hopscotch every day and then suddenly a complete change to rounders, why the sudden changes occurred was inexplicable. Also how we knew that the corn harvest was starting was a mystery.

Maybe we saw Dickie Jones or Watty

Holmes going down the village with a scythe over their shoulder. They would be going to make the first cut around the cornfield to give the binder room to work. Maybe Laurie's brother would tell us, but one day we would select sticks from the hedge and set to preparing them.

Normally they were ash branches, broken off from the trunk of the tree to leave a knob on the end. These would be trimmed free of twigs, cut to length, and then we would sit carving the bark into diamonds, bands and spirals. Next day we four boys (or 'young shavers' to the locals) would be off on our bikes, with our sticks, down through the village and over Barn Hill to the field by Granny Shappie's Lane at Bratton Cross, which was normally the first field to be cut.

We would frequently arrive too early, dump our bikes in the hedge and sit waiting. The corn would be a lovely golden colour, rustling in the breeze. In the early days it was usually oats, then the farmers started to grow wheat or what we called 'Bearded Barley', we did not approve of this as the awns were sharp and really pricked you and stuck in your socks.

Buster would usually produce a copy of the 'Health and Efficiency' magazine, which he bought with his pocket money, and we would all examine the airbrushed pictures of the nudists to catch a glimpse of a naked female breast. We would also consume any lunch that we had brought, washed down with pop, our young appetites not permitting us to wait until midday.

As there was no such thing as a combine harvester then, a strip as wide as the tractor would have been cut by hand the day before completely around the field. The farmer, or a farm worker, would have done this with a scythe, gathering all the corn and tying it into sheaves with a twisted rope made out of corn stalks. These sheaves were propped up against the field hedge out of harms way.

Soon, when the sun had dried the dew off the corn we would hear the sound of a tractor approaching. We would open the gate and the tractor would swing into the field pulling the binder which was on its tyred road wheels and was being towed sideways with its flail wheel collapsed.

The tractor would park in a cleared area just inside the gate and two men would dismount. One was normally Ronnie Squire, who drove the tractor, the other may have been Pat Sage, Reg Symonds (nicknamed

Rattleboots for some unknown reason), or sometimes the farmer who owned the field.

They would start by winding down the big steel centre wheel of the Binder, moving the tractor around and attaching it to the front of the Binder. They would then remove the Binder's road wheels and attach a steel rimmed wheel to the end of the binder bed, also erecting the flail wheel.

Shortly, from our position, lying against the hedge, we would watch the tractor driver take his place and the binder operator climb up onto his seat behind and above the bed. From this position he could control the height of the flail wheel and ensure the cut corn was falling correctly on to the bed. He would also keep an eye on the discharged sheaves to make sure they were tied properly.

We would not move yet as, this being the first cut of the season, we would anticipate the forthcoming problems. After a jerky start, as the cutters went in to the first swathe of corn and the binder operator lowered his handle to lower the flail wheel and engage the cutters, there would be a cry of 'Whoa' as the first sheaf emerged, untied, from the binder. All would stop, and great consternation ensued as they dismounted and re-threaded the binder cord and cleaned the winter's accumulation of rust off the knotting mechanism.

Soon a re-mount of both operatives and a restart, probably stopping again immediately for either further adjustments, or tightening the bed belt. There would be further stops on the first round to clear the remains of a mole 'heave' or mouse's nest off the cutter fingers.

We would not normally stir ourselves until they had managed at least one successful round of the field. Even then, knowing the ways of our furry friends, we were loath to accompany the combination around the field, but one of us would draw the short straw and walk out to meet the binder as it passed.

This unfortunate, balancing his stick on his shoulder, would catch hold of the pipe supporting the seat on which the binder operator sat and walk around the field watching the edge of the corn with no great expectation of results. As he completed the circuit he would peel off and resume his seat at the hedge, his place being taken by the next volunteer.

This process would continue for the first few rounds of the field, eventually the monotony being broken by the cry of 'Hoo Loo, Loo, Loo', from a distant part of the field, indicating that the first rabbit had broken cover from the diminishing corn and was heading for the hedge.

This caused a change in outlook of those remaining by the hedge and we now vied with each other to be the next to follow the binder. It also heralded the arrival in the field of the farmer and one of his men who were going to 'stook' the corn.

This 'stooking' entailed grabbing two sheaves and standing them on end, propped against each other, followed by two more at right angles forming a 'stook' of four. This allowed the corn not only to dry, but assisted in protecting it against rain, should it not be brought to the rick or stack for a few days. This 'stooking' is not to be confused with 'pooking' a somewhat similar operation already explained and applied to hay.

Stooks may still be seen in cornfields today. Sometimes a binder is used instead of a Combine Harvester, to avoid breaking the straw, so it may be used for thatching. Stooking is then still employed to protect it against the elements.

The rabbits, as they emerged from the standing corn, would run towards the hedge but never in straight lines, whether distracted by our cries of 'Hoo, Loo, Loo', or whether just to put us off we did not know, but their zigzag path enabled us to gain on them. A well aimed blow with our stick either dispatched them immediately, or stunned them so that a quick yank on the neck completed their demise. We then carried them back to our resting-place and deposited them in the hedge.

As the amount of standing corn got less two of us at a time would accompany the binder around and the chases became more hectic, dodging amongst the increasing number of stooks being erected. Eventually the remaining corn would be of such a size that the passage of the binder down one side might frighten the rabbits out of the other.

When this situation prevailed we would all leave our resting-place and take up station on each side of the remaining stand of corn.

The 'Hoo Loo Loos' became more frequent, egged on by the tractor driver and his mate, and we would be flying around the field after the rabbits, some making good their escape but even more falling to our sticks.

It was quite amazing that even when the remaining corn stand had reduced so that we could see through it, or even reach across it, there would still be rabbits cowering within it, and emerging at frequent intervals. In fact until the last straws had bent over under the flail wheel we could not be certain of the end of our sport.

We would then repair to our place beside the hedge and count our booty. Sometimes two or more of us would claim the same quarry but we always managed to distribute them amicably, sometimes the more successful hunter giving some to the less successful. Occasionally the farmer himself would demand a share, this we denigrated and held such men in ill odour.

There were even a few who confiscated the whole haul. Wallace Heal was one of these selfish farmers, which we found out the first time we visited Rye Park, but we managed to hide one or two from him and retrieve them later. We never went to his farm again in subsequent years.

Before leaving the field we would slit one leg of our quarry with a knife, and insert the other back leg through the hole so that we could hang them on the handlebars of our bikes. Usually, if it had been a good haul, we would intertwine the legs of two in order to produce a 'Brace'.

Our booty went in many directions, some home to be paunched, skinned and

119

cooked for the family tomorrow. Some to be paunched, have a piece of brown paper wrapped around the slit, a stamped luggage label tied to the back leg, and be dispatched to our meat rationed friends in London.

The rest we sold to Mr Lerwill, who would pay us the princely sum of one shilling (5p) per bunny. These were either re-sold in his shop or sent on to Percy Brend in Butchers Row, Barnstaple, who sent large consignments by train to London.

We would cycle slowly home, up Barn Hill and then through the village, discussing the possibilities of the next field due to be cut on the morrow. Tired, but we were happy at the thought of our family's pleasure at a meat meal, in those days of strict rationing. Also we were happy at the possibility of some extra pocket money.

The only injury sustained on these forays, I believe, was to me. It was at Beara, farmed by a very friendly farmer, Mr Thorne, when, in an excess of zeal I chased a large rat instead of a rabbit. The rat took shelter under a sheaf and I grabbed it by the tail, holding it aloft to whack its head with my stick.

Before I had achieved this it had lifted itself up on its tail and sunk its teeth into the back of my hand. Much wailing, and as the

bite turned septic, many hot Kaolin poultices,
to draw the poison, applied by Nurse Moor.

Chapter 14

The Church

The top churchyard wall, on the railings, was a favourite meeting place of ours and the planning office for many of our escapades. We would also use it as a viewing platform whilst watching the internment of some poor soul in the graveyard.

Our Favourite Perch

The two yew trees at this entrance formed a place of concealment for our small bodies when escaping from retribution for some infraction of the rules in the Hall opposite. Just inside the gate on the right were the two graves with glass domes, under which we would obtain our Slow Worms.

At the bottom of the Churchyard under the tall trees was a large rubbish dump. Whether this had been formed by occupants of the Alms houses, or by previous occupants of Craigside throwing rubbish over the paddock hedge, was unknown. Whoever did it must have had a peculiar diet, and suffered from it, as a large proportion of the dump consisted of Marmite jars and Milk of Magnesia bottles I remember.

There were many dumps like this around houses, as there was no rubbish collection, what could not be burned had to be dumped, often into Devon Banks when they were constructed, or down rabbit holes. In later years we often found antique bottles etc. when demolishing these Banks.

The trees at one time housed a rookery, the noise of which annoyed us at Craigside. The rooks were eradicated by Rex, using father's shotgun, from our field.

In this area also, Fred used to burn the rubbish when he cleaned the churchyard. It was rumoured that when digging new graves he often came across bones of previous unmarked ones. It was said that these were burned along with the rubbish and my parents sometimes joked that they would end up on Fred's bonfire.

When it rained we often took shelter in the church porch or in the church itself which was never locked. Church services were much more popular in those days and Sundays held in more reverence. We boys were normally not allowed out to play on a Sunday.

On Sunday afternoons we all had to attend the Sunday school in the church. We did not view this restriction with relish and I think Rev. Cave-Moyle spent as much time controlling us as teaching us the scriptures.

After Sunday school, if the weather was clement we would go for a walk down by Button River or around the Triangle with our parents. In the evenings we would attend Evensong with our families. Normally each family would keep to the same pew for every visit. Although there was no right of ownership of any particular pew, by the black looks received, you would be left in no doubt if you had usurped someone else's usual seat.

When not forced to visit the church we would do so of our own volition, on many occasions. Fred Bale would allow us to sit quietly on a winters evening in the Ringing

Chamber to watch the ringers practising.

Fred Bale, Jack Folkes, Alfie Squire, George Tribe
Arthur Clarke and Lionel Bale

He kept the door to the tower locked, but the key, attached to a red cotton reel, hung by the door. We would climb the tower and take the key with us to stop anyone locking the door while we were up.

The stone staircase up the tower was very narrow and especially so as you passed the Belfry, necessitating some contortions at that point. The bells, when not in use, were left in the inverted position resting in their wooden frames. The operating ropes in the

Ringing Chamber were always looped up and tied out of the reach of little hands. Surely they did not think we would pull them, did they? The view from the top of the tower is very impressive and we boys would often climb it to survey the surrounding countryside.

One moonlit night my mother was returning from a WI meeting in the Village Hall. She took her usual shortcut through the churchyard, down to the Alms houses and up the lane to Craigside.

As she was passing through the churchyard she heard her name called in a deep voice. She peered around at the gravestones thinking someone was hiding there. The voice came again saying, "It is no good looking there, this is your maker calling".

My mother, although obeying certain superstitions like not allowing knives to be crossed or not picking up a knife if you were the one that dropped it, was not a really superstitious lady. She also did not believe in ghosts, but she said the hairs on the back of her neck stood up at the sound of this supernatural voice and again stopped and looked everywhere.

Eventually, sounds of laughter reached

her from Fred, who was on the top of the tower. He had gone to wind the clock and as it was such a beautiful night had carried on up to the top to appreciate the view. I do not think my mother ever forgave him for her fright.

The bells were not rung at one period during the war as the sound was to be used to herald a German invasion of England. However I do remember one day being down below Vickery's fields in Bratton woods and hearing the sad tolling of the Tenor bell. It was always rung to signify the death of the oldest village inhabitant. One stroke for every year of their life, I wonder if this custom still persists.

The clock mechanism was very prone to failure and its hands were stationary for months at a time. My mother wrote an amusing poem that was reproduced in the North Devon Journal.

The Old Lady of Bratton

In Bratton she with us did dwell
Always a faithful friend.
With bated breath we watch her yet;
Surely 'tis not the end.

Both man and maid since infant days
Have looked to her alone
To tell them right; from morn 'till night.
She's watched them from her throne.

Her hands that worked for friend or foe,
And never worked in vain,
Is it to be that those dear hands
Will never work again?

It's sad to see her helpless plight,
Bereft of all her power.
What is this trouble which involves
Our clock in the Church Tower?

All this religious education left little impression on us boys. In fact one Monday morning at school, the day after Harvest Festival, I was called up in front of Sam's desk. He asked me what I knew about the disappearance of most of the luscious fruits that had adorned the altar in the church on the Saturday, but were not there on the Sunday.

On this occasion I was truthfully able to plead ignorance as it was my first day out of isolation with Chicken Pox and I had not been near the church. I did know the perpetrators but wild horses would not drag their names from my lips. They were not all from Bratton.

There was only one refuge for us during Sunday services and that was the Vestry. We vied with each other to be the operator of the organ pump there.

The organ was supplied by bellows operated by the long handle of the pump, as were many church organs at that time. One of us would be chosen to sit on a chair in the vestry and operate this. On many occasions the organist would depress the keys for the opening bars of a hymn to find that a squeak was the only result. This caused a call of "Wake up Boy" followed by the sound of energetic pumping and a forced change of operator for the next service.

Later, George Tribe started a hand bell group. They performed at various village functions and venues. The photograph shows the founder members.

George is the only survivor at this time. David Barrow was unfortunately killed subsequently in a car accident in Wiltshire. His brother Curly was riding pillion when Ginger Squire had his terrible accident, but luckily he escaped with only minor injuries. Both of the Barrow brothers were at one time honorary members of our gang. Derek Marshall and Raymond Bennett died some years ago.

David Barrow, Buster, Derek Marshall and George
The Hand bell Ringers

Chapter 15

Gaumont British Junior Club

Laurie remembers my Father having a grey Ford Prefect FYO39, but in fact the first car he used to take us to Barum in was a black Morris 12, CLY780, which is irrelevant, but this one had an interesting history. Father had a garage in London S & B's, 'Smith and Becketts', and sold cars.

However, the bottom fell out of the used car market at the start of the war and Father was left with several cars on his hands, one of which was the Morris and another a large green Chrysler. We used the Chrysler ourselves and Dad sold the Morris to the daughter of the family at Kittytoe for £12. As part of the deal he also had to teach her to drive it!

Being a salesman it really hurt him to make such a loss and, when later he saw it for sale in Elliot's garage in Lynton he traded in the Chrysler for it, and it came to Bratton. In fact he bought and sold that car four times over the years until he had cleared a profit on it. However, I digress, and regardless of the vehicle involved let's get back to the main story.

Apart from the Village Hall there was little entertainment in the village. We had the radio and we had a piano, but it was not my idea of fun to stand around it in the evening singing 'The Quartermaster's Stores' with my sister and cousin. One day Father took me to work with him on a Saturday morning and dropped me off at the Gaumont cinema for the pictures. I was absolutely in heaven during the films. The Lone Ranger etc.

For the next week I really upset the other three by pointing my fingers and going 'Bang, bang', and shouting 'Heigh Ho Silver'. The next week I asked Dad if Pat could come too, and we both then really annoyed Laurie and Buster with our continual cowboy antics. However the following week I asked Dad if all four of us could go, and that was the start of our entertainment on Saturdays for the remainder of the war.

We would all meet at Craigside and spend the journey wondering what the main film would be. We had a cartoon, an episode of a serial, and a main film each week. The usual ones I remember are 'Roy Rogers' and 'The Lone Ranger'. I don't know how girl members felt, as I think they were mainly cowboy films, apart from several about 'The Bowery Boys', Norman Wisdom, silent ones with Buster Keaton, and one about the D day invasion.

We all had membership cards for the club and, although it was the Gaumont, I seem to remember many times queuing outside the Regal in the Strand with the queue stretching up a narrow alleyway beside it. We used to wonder if we would get in. The programme always started with Uncle Bob Sawyer giving out notices, especially of birthdays, on which you went up into the Circle and could take one friend.

We all sang 'Happy birthday to you', and then had community singing with the words on the screen and a bouncing ball to keep us in time. 'Lily of Laguna', 'Isle of Capri' and 'You are my Sunshine', being the usual favourites although we frequently substituted our own words to the tunes.

During this singing the birthday boys in the circle threw anything they could lay their hands on down onto their fellows in the stalls. We always concluded with the first verse of the National Anthem, the last line of which went "God save our, on with the Show"! I still can never hear the Anthem, even on the most serious occasions, without remembering that.

We were always spellbound with the

films, they were very real to us, magical, Popeye, Mickey, Donald etc. Then the serious serial, the possible outcome of which had been our topic of conversation the previous week, followed by the main feature. We were always sad to emerge into the daylight from this escapism, but the mornings delights were still not over.

Normally we had pocket money to spend, no such delights as sweets, rationed and bought in Bratton, or Ice Creams. Fortes on the square was firmly shut for the duration of the war but we used to look at the china replicas of ice creams gathering dust in the window. No, it was Mortimer's, in Boutport Street opposite the Gaumont, for fireworks. Jumping Jacks or Little Demon bangers, or a long blue tin of carbide to make our own.

At other times it was down the High Street to Woolworths. Sample purchases were a new supply of caps, little lead bombs in two halves tied with string to contain a cap, pistols made out of wire and spring.

A red and yellow string telephone set, (that Laurie and I rigged between our bedroom windows but it failed us over the two hundred yards). A tin whistle affair that you hummed into and it gave musical notes. Bubble blowing kits, Bird warblers, etc. Later we would visit Gales the gunsmiths in High Street for cartridges or fishing tackle.

We would then go either to the river wall, by the square, to watch the river for a while or wend our way back to the County Garage where Father had his office. Sometimes we would call in at Lakes the drapers, opposite the end of Bear Street, to watch the serving girls send the payments to the cashier by a little overhead railway and receive the change by the same method. This shop was the only one in Barnstaple to have such a mechanism.

Father might be working at the Central Garage on the Square, or Prideaux's in Bear Street as they both sub-contracted work. He was in charge of Quality Control for army vehicle repair, eventually for all garages west of a line from Bristol to Bournemouth. But on Saturdays he always went to his office in the County and we would go to the car park there to wait for him.

The car park was always full of Matador searchlight towing lorries, armoured troop carriers, Bren gun carriers, jeeps and every describable army vehicle, which we used to examine with great interest, and frequently climb all over them until turfed off by some officious garage hand.

Father used to take these out on test drives, frequently calling in at Bratton en route and you could often see most peculiar vehicles like DUKWS parked in Craigside drive. These amphibious vehicles were tested on Braunton and Saunton sands.

A DUKW

At one time most of the vehicles were destined for the North Africa campaign and were in desert camouflage. I noticed their steering wheels all had a small piece of white tape in one position. I asked Dad about this and was told that it stopped them going in circles in the desert at night, if they just kept the tape at the top of the wheel they would go straight ahead.

Then the twenty minute drive back to

Bratton, how Dad managed to concentrate with our continual chatter, let alone the games we used to play, Rock breaks Scissors, Paper covers Rock, Scissors cut Paper followed by knuckle raps. The other one, equally vicious, where you place your hands on the upturned palms of your opponents and try to remove them before getting slapped.

He used to enter into the spirit of it though, and I remember one time that Buster hid his eyes and said he would tell us when we got to the top of the Turnpike by Granny Shappie's Lane.

Buster failed in his attempt, and we were nearly at the top of Barn Hill when he said 'Now'. What Buster had noticed on previous trips was that Father always changed gear at the top of Turnpike, but on this occasion Father, realising what was going on, deliberately delayed the gear change.

Saturday afternoons normally consisted of re-enactments of plots witnessed in the morning, often around the uninhabited Alms houses, using their steps as a mountain.

Chapter 16

Food and Farming

These were the war years and strict food and clothing rationing was in force. Whilst the clothes rationing affected us, as it did the townies, food rationing did not bite quite so deeply. Most farms were self sufficient in most foodstuffs and those unobtainable locally could be bartered for items that were. This was not considered blackmarketeering.

There were restrictions imposed upon us, for example hoarding food was illegal and a licence was required to kill your own pig. Sometimes these were ignored but a strict watch was kept by the local bobby, PC Chapman, who was rumoured to creep up garden paths at night and peer through larder windows with the aid of his torch.

We kept cows, which provided our milk, butter and cream, with enough surpluses to barter. Mother would set a large aluminium pan of milk to scald on the gas stove each day. This would then be transferred to the inner pantry to stand and cool on the slate shelf.

By the next morning the top of the milk

would be covered with a thick layer of solid yellow clotted cream. Mother would use a fish slice to roll the cream across the surface like a Swiss roll and lift it into a dish. I still prefer this to the white smooth substance sold in many supermarket outlets these days purporting to be 'Clotted Cream'.

The milk remaining in the pan was quite thin, but had many flecks of solid cream remaining in it, this we called skimmed milk, again quite different from that sold by the milkman of today. It was lovely to drink and my friends and I would be given a glass of it and a slice of cake, mid morning at weekends and holidays. When we went on all day rambles we would take it in preference to pop on occasions.

One thing Mother never made was butter but she passed our extra milk over the hedge to Watty Holmes' wife who would convert it into a large roll of yellow butter formed with wooden butter pats. At one time Father bought a motorised milk separator but, if my memory serves me correctly we never used this.

Nearly everyone kept chickens of course which meant a plentiful supply of eggs. What most Townies do not realise is that chickens do not lay all the year round but only in days of increasing daylight.

Of course these days in poultry houses they can be fooled by judicious use of electric lights but we had no electricity, so they obeyed nature. To overcome this deficit we had large galvanised pans in the outer pantry, under the shelves. Mother bought water-glass, and diluted it in water to fill the pans. Into these went the eggs for preserving, and they kept in good condition for use during the months when the hens were out of lay.

We allowed some chickens to sit their own eggs. Although they were encouraged to lay in the nesting boxes, by the presence of a china egg, many chose to lay away in the paddock hedges, especially the Bantams.

They were very crafty, and having laid they would go some distance away before making their "I've laid an egg", call. It was one of my jobs to scour the hedges to discover the miscreants before they could go broody and start sitting to hatch chicks. If not found the eggs or chicks would normally fall prey to rats or weasels that managed to evade the farmyard cat.

Sometimes, however, a wily old bird would appear leading a few chicks behind her. Old birds that had finished laying were called Boilers and were cooked, mainly for stock, but if boiled well would be tender enough for a hungry mouth. Cock birds, and some pullets not required for the laying flock, would supplement the meat ration.

When a hen sat in the nesting box all day, and was so dopey that she could be lifted off and replaced with no protest, Mother would know she had gone broody. She would give her a box to herself and thirteen eggs to sit.

When they started to hatch, over a few days, Mother would remove the chicks one by one, to stop the hen leaving the nest and the remainder of the eggs, to go off with her early offspring. Mother would put them in a lined basket and hang it beside the kitchen range to keep them warm.

They were fed, cannibal like, on chopped up hard boiled egg, normally on newspaper on the kitchen table, until the hatch was complete and they were strong enough to be returned to their mother.

I remember one time I had chicken pox and was confined to bed at hatching time. Mother brought in a basket of chicks to cheer me up and I lifted one or two onto the bed. One chick must have thought one of my scabs was an ear of corn as it pecked it off and ate it. I still have the scar on my arm sixty odd years later.

In earlier years farm labourers in tied cottages always had a sty at the rear of their cottage. They were allowed, as part of their remuneration, to keep a pig for their own consumption and look to the farm produce, and that of their own garden, for its keep.

During the war many people, not just farmers, adopted this idea and kept pigs. We usually had two and fed them on corn, skimmed milk and vegetable waste, but got the butcher to deal with them when the time was ripe.

Pat's father on the other hand kept one at a time at the bottom of their large garden. This one was dealt with in situ when it reached maturity. These days the housewife demands and gets lean pork and pigs are graded by the thickness of the outer layer of fat, with a penalty price if this is too great. This means they are killed earlier, classed as baconers or porkers, but in those days the idea was to get the pig as big and as fat as possible. They therefore had an immense amount of fat on them.

When the time came, several women including Freddie Shapland's mother from next door, would congregate in Pat's mother's wash house, boiling water in the copper and scrupulously cleaning the stone work surfaces. One or two men would come to help his father, bringing a pig table. This was a wooden, low, narrow, stretcher like table with two handles each end.

They would carry this up to the sty and despatch the pig with a pig sticker, something like a knife sharpening steel. Having bled the pig they would bring it, on the pig table, to the bottom of the garden outside the wash house, where we boys would be waiting to watch the hard work.

Having washed the pig thoroughly in cold water they would then pour boiling water over it. Armed with scrapers that looked like inverted funnels, with the inside of the large end possessing a circular sharp blade, they would shave the pig. They would then butcher it and pass the joints in to the women. The entrails were thoroughly scrubbed inside and out and set aside for later making the skins of Hogs Pudding. This consisted of the meat scraps from ears cheeks etc., mixed with barley and seasoning and cooked as sausages.

Mrs Parkhouse used to make the most delicious Hogs Pudding I ever tasted, not a bit like today's mass produced sausages. In later years my father saw me peeling the skin off a sausage and asked me why I did it, I said I didn't like eating plastic. He averred that it was pig's intestine and was quite amazed when I told him that these days it was bought as edible plastic tube by the mile. He never ate a sausage skin after that.

Other scraps of meat, especially from head and trotters were used to make a delicious Brawn. This nutritious jellified substance was either eaten cold with vegetables at a main meal, or between bread as a sandwich.

Of course we had no refrigerators then, so the women were busy salting down the prepared joints in earthenware troughs for salt pork or bacon. Large pieces of the fat would be salted separately and these when fried referred to as 'Fat Back' which, placed between two slabs of bread, made a nourishing and warming breakfast.

Nowadays worries about cholesterol would stop anyone eating it, just as bread and dripping has faded out, but in those days we thought it was very good for you.

About this stage of the proceedings we boys would be presented with the bladder. This inflated, when the three tubes were tied off, would either go inside a leather football case if one was available, as rubber bladders were unobtainable, or be used as a football in its natural state.

Much bartering went on for any fresh joints and many houses in the village had a great Sunday lunch that week. There is a world of difference between the taste of today's mass produced pork, raised on pig nuts, and that raised on vegetable waste, table scraps and milk. This was especially so when the pigs were allowed to free range in pens attached to the sty.

It was always said that the only thing a pig had that could not be used was the squeal.

As regards other meat, I have already mentioned rabbits of course, which were plentiful, but some lambs and bullocks seemed to get lost from the herd or flock on some farms. On the whole the true country people did not go unrewarded for their labour to keep the townspeople fed. Turkeys and geese were also kept, with the other poultry, so Christmas and Michaelmas were celebrated in traditional style.

We did see National Dried Milk but we mainly used the tins for keeping things in, dried egg also came in for baking on occasions, concentrated orange juice for the children and the much hated Cod Liver Oil and Malt. Fruit, apart from citrus was plentiful, both the cultivated and wild varieties, so jam making was a popular pastime. Without refrigeration preserving fruit in Kilner jars was a necessity, the problem being to obtain replacement rubber sealing rings for them.

One particularly tasty fruit was Whortleberry or Whorts (pronounced wertz) as they are called in Devon. These grow in abundance around the village and on the outskirts of Exmoor especially above North Molton. They grow on very small bushes and picking them is backbreaking work, unless you can find a Devon bank covered with them. This permits you to pick them standing up.

The picking is so time consuming as after hours you would have only picked a small basin full, and your fingers would be stained purple, that few people bother picking in today's affluent society.

In the season you can still find a few punnets of Whortleberries on sale in Barnstaple Pannier Market today, but in those days there were scores of pickers prepared to work hard for the few pence they would achieve in the Market. Some locals, particularly Charlie Clarke and his wife, used a mechanical invention to speed the picking.

This consisted of an open ended

wooden trough with nails driven through the base, spaced about a quarter of an inch apart, and protruding some four inches at the front. This device collected a lot of leaves as it was passed through the bush but also masses of Whorts for sale.

We were always out picking when they were ripe as Mother would make a delicious Summer Pudding with them, in a bread lined basin with a saucer on top pressed down under the weight of a flat iron. Eaten with cream it was the best pudding I ever tasted.

Something else I have not tasted since the war years is Yeast Cake. Not being a cook I have little idea of the recipe but remember Mother putting yeast into warm milk and mixing it into dough with flour. It would then stand in front of the range in a basin, with a cloth over it, to 'prove' or 'rise' before being formed into cakes and baked.

If they were available, raisins would be added to the mix, and the yeasty smell of it baking was mouth-watering. Sliced and buttered with farmhouse butter it melted in your mouth.

Laurie's mother's speciality to my mind was her 'Teddy Cake', obviously potatoes formed a large part of the constituents but it was produced as a golden brown flat sweet cake eaten cold. I remember many times calling for Laurie to come out and play on a summers evening and his mother, knowing my weakness would say, "We are just having tea and there's Teddy Cake would you like some". I would join them at table and gorge myself.

This did cause problems at times as Laurie then was an inveterate giggler. I would only have to raise an eyebrow to set him off, to the exasperation of his family.

All my three friends used to come to my house for tea frequently and in the summer Mother would serve us outside under the Holly tree. However in the winter when I asked her if they could come she would say, "Laurie can come only if he promises not to giggle".

Vegetables, we seemed to be able to store over winter in those days, whereas today they seem to rot in a few weeks. Mangolds for the sheep and cattle were kept in the field buried under heaps of earth called 'Clamps'. This method was also used for swedes and turnips.

Carrots were kept in a shed in sand, or under straw, as were potatoes. We ate, or in my case did not eat, all sorts of 'Greens', some of which seem to have been discovered by the gourmets of today as new delicacies, but to us then they were staple foods. No frozen food for us in those days. Everyone had a vegetable garden and all the propaganda exhorted us to 'Dig for Victory', meaning grow as much of your own food as you can, and we did just that.

Many farms had a cider apple orchard and possessed their own cider press. Part of a farm workers due in those days was his lunch time cider, and more often than lunchtime at haymaking. No farm would be able to get decent labour if they did not offer this facility. The Scrumpy then bore little resemblance to the Scrumpy of today. Homemade, it varied from farm to farm.

I have heard of pieces of pork being thrown in to the fermenting vats to dissolve in the acid contents giving it body, and even tales of rats caught in the cider shed being thrown in.

I have seen cider being drawn from a wooden barrel and, in the pouring, a stoppage occurring. I have seen the barman then pull the end of a long string of undissolved fat from the tap to restore the flow. I have drunk it, and would advise anyone unaccustomed to real 'Scrumpy' to limit themselves in the first instance to a half a pint, although the farm workers would drink it by the gallon.

Chapter 17

Shops and Services

There were only four or five cars in the village and petrol rationing limited the use of even these. The only way to Barnstaple therefore, was by pony and trap or the Southern National bus.

The bus service was also hampered by fuel rationing and various other types of fuel were tried, in particular gas. The first trial was with a balloon, secured to the top of the bus, filled with gas. Unfortunately nobody took account of the overhanging trees near Chelfam and the ensuing puncture of the balloon brought the journey to an abrupt end.

Next try was with a gas container attached to the rear of the bus in a trailer. The inefficient use of the gas, by an engine designed for diesel, caused such a reduction in power that it was almost impossible for the bus to grind its way up Bratton and Grange Hill so the idea was abandoned.

Because of the paucity of transport the village was far better off for services then than now. The General Store was referred to as Lower Shop, situated on the corner of Haxton Lane. This was run by two families, Norman and Woolacott in the early years, before being taken over by the Whites, and later by the Cockbills. As is usual with a general store it sold most things and we bought our sweet ration and pop there.

Lower Shop with Petrol Pumps

This shop also housed the Post Office which had moved down from its previous situation at the entrance to Rectory Lane. Outside the shop stood two hand operated petrol pumps. When there was petrol available the shopkeeper would serve it by rotating a handle which worked a lift pump. The upward stroke would deliver half a gallon a time.

In the centre of the village was the Bakery, operated by George Ewens assisted by one of his sons, Fred. George's wife, Granny Ewens, served in the shop which as well as bakery items sold sweets, sugar when available on ration, and various other commodities including cigarettes, again when available.

Fred, Granny, George and Bill Ewens

Granny Ewens was a lovely old lady and always had time for a chat to all customers, including us boys. If we had a few coppers to spare we would visit her because she always gave us overweight on anything we bought or would throw in a hot new baked bun from George's bakery.

The Bakery

We would buy our England's Glory red top matches from her to make our fires or explosives, and she never questioned why we wanted them, or later, when we bought open packets of five Woodbines, having graduated from dried grass in newspaper.

My mother was always sending me there with a list of groceries and insisted, on my return, that I tell her the price of each item and count out the correct change. She considered this good discipline for me and a help to improve my arithmetic.

Unfortunately Granny Ewens' arithmetic was not much better than mine and it was rare that the tally would satisfy mother. I would be sent back to the shop to be greeted by Granny saying "Oh dear David, did we get it wrong again?" followed by a recalculation involving much licking of the pencil.

One of our favourite buys was Cherry Linctus cough drops which were not on ration, although in short supply. Granny would weigh out a pennyworth and pour them into a little triangular paper bag twisting the top closed. When we were very hungry, which was often, as young boys are, we would buy one of Georges fresh baked loaves and sit on the wall outside the shop and share it out.

George was always very kindly disposed towards us boys. I suppose he considered that, although we were tearaways, we were probably not as much trouble as his own son Fred, and our pranks were no worse than Fred's, even when Fred had reached adulthood.

George would welcome us into his bakery to see him mixing the dough in a large rotating steel drum, kneading and proving it in a large wooden trough and then tinning it into loaves which he inserted into the ovens with a long handled shovel. I never thought to ask what powered the drum or fired the ovens, was it a petrol engine and bottled gas respectively I wonder.

George produced the most delicious bread and would deliver it around the village in a large rectangular wicker basket, covered with a cloth, over his arm. It was a sad day for the village when he retired and the Bakery was bought by North Devon Bakeries, with the express purpose of closing it, so that they could sell their own bread.

I still think it tragic when the multinationals buy up village facilities in order to close them. This is how we lost the wonderful 'Bluebell Line', the Barnstaple to Lynton narrow gauge railway, bought by the bus company and closed in 1935 for fear of the competition.

Fred and Dulcie Ewens had a new house next to the shop with a workshop behind it. Fred erected a windmill there with a generator attached and used it to recharge the numerous accumulators which the village used to power radios and lights. The tail of this windmill became a great attraction to us when we eventually acquired air rifles, much to Fred's chagrin.

Fred told me one day, how he sold a radio to a farmer who returned a few days later saying it would not work. When Fred took the back off he found it to be full of tractor engine oil. When he queried the farmer the answer was "Yes, it was squeaking so I oiled un".

Rosemarie

I remember Dulcie giving birth to a

daughter, Rosemarie, and on hearing the news I ran home excitedly and burst out to Mother "Mrs Ewens has had a baby, not old Mrs Ewens, young Mrs Ewens", which caused a certain amount of mirth as Granny must have been in her seventies. Rosemarie later married Arthur, the younger brother of one of my classmates Vera Ridd-Jones.

Fred was quite a character. He kept bees and not being a cricket lover, and not liking the noise when a game was being played on the pitch behind his house, would stir up the hives to see the cricketers run for cover from the angry swarm.

The story is also told of the time Art Heal was transporting some hives up the road on his cart for Fred. After they had loaded the hives and Art remounted, Fred gave a hive a mighty thump. The bees stung the horse and it set off up the road at high speed. Fred split his sides laughing. Art did not regain control of the horse until he reached Bill Dallyn's farm. PC Chapman missed his chance of issuing a speeding ticket for Art's cart.

Next to Fred's house was the Blacksmith's owned by Jim Lavercombe. He was kept very busy shoeing horses and mending farm machinery in addition to making ironwork for the villagers.

Fred's House and Bakery from Tower

On rainy or cold days we would often visit him to watch him at work, as the Smithy was always warmed by the forge. He was a nice old chap who would often let us boys pump the bellows while he worked at the forge heating the iron.

We were always assured of a welcome from Jim although the same could not be said of his son Alfie, who worked for the Fanshawes at Holywell. It was not unknown for Alfie to use his twelve bore to frighten us, when chasing us, having caught us trespassing or scrumping apples in the grounds.

Opposite the Smithy was The White Hart pub run by Jim Kemble. His son Jack together with John Orchard eventually ran the garage that replaced the Smithy.

White Hart

Jim Lavercombe lived next door to the butchers. The butchers shop was owned by Mr Lerwill, who had a son, Peter, slightly older than us. It was one of the few houses in the village with a lawn, on which we were allowed to play at times. Behind the lawn was a garage, full of massive empty Corned Beef tins. Corned Beef was the main commodity sold in the butcher's and, if my memory serves me right, even that was rationed.

Mr Lerwill would purchase any rabbits we caught, for resale, so we boys knew him quite well. There was always a queue outside his shop when there was a delivery of meat.

Mr Lerwill used to borrow our old sheepdog, Bruce, when he went to see some sheep which he kept near Four Cross Ways. We understood that he took the dog there and back in his van but would let him out by his shop and he would trot home.

One day the dog came back completely exhausted lay down and passed away. We then found out that he had always made him run, there and back, behind his van and also work hard all day. I never forgave him for that.

We often used to sit chatting on the narrow windowsill outside the large shop window. I think it was Laurie's brother who leaned back one day and cracked the glass right across, but I think we youngsters got the blame.

Next door but one to the butchers was Laurie's house. The front room of his house was rented to a cobbler, Bill Merrett. Bill used to bicycle or, when he could get the petrol, motorcycle out to Bratton from Barnstaple everyday. Unfortunately later in life he was killed on his motorcycle on the Braunton road. He was a great character and always welcomed us into his shop.

I think from the hours I spent standing next to Bill, as he worked on his last, I could have become a cobbler myself. He not only repaired shoes and re-studded boots but actually made them from scratch. He had a large treadle operated polishing and grinding machine with which we boys would love to play but, with the welfare of the belts in mind, he would ask us to desist.

One day Pat and Laurie so exasperated Bill that he chased them out of the shop and threw after them a bucket of brown stinking water in which he had been soaking leather. They managed to dodge it, but Gordon Ward, who was innocently passing in the road, received the whole bucketful. Pat and Laurie were not contrite but actually, to their lasting shame, somewhat amused. Bill was later admonished by Gordon's mother Jess Ward, for sending home an evil smelling son.

Bill, in a good mood, would regale us with risqué songs, poems and jokes as he worked, and any facts of life which we did not learn in the countryside we certainly learned from him. He also provided us with the small nails or 'sprigs' needed for our attempts at French Knitting.

One phrase he used puzzled me for a long time, when I was very young. He would refer to all ladies high heeled shoes that came in for repair as horse shoes, they did not look similar to me. It was when I was a little more mature that I found out he meant whores shoes.

Bill Merrett

Opposite Bill Merrett's was the carpenters workshop owned by Harold Parkin who lived in a house behind it. This was another house with a large lawn but the only time we were allowed on that one was when we were invited to his daughter Margaret's birthday party. I do remember there being a wasp's nest in the bottom hedge of the garden, where the party was held. I, of course, could not leave well alone, and had to stir it up with a stick.

I had warned Pat to move away but he stayed sitting on the lawn facing the nest. The obvious happened and out flew a wasp and stung him on the eyelid. This necessitated a trip across the road to Bills for the application of a Reckitts blue bag. Bill always had a supply as he kept bees in Laurie's garden.

Harold's Workshop minus veranda

Over the big window outside Harold's workshop was a slate veranda. Under here we used to congregate when it rained, or on a dark winters evening, when it would be lit by the oil lamps in the workshop. We were not very popular with Harold on several counts. He had a petrol engine providing power for his circular saw just inside the gate to the Splat.

One of our tricks was to block the exhaust which either caused it to stop or make it impossible to start. I believe he was also in no doubt that it was Laurie and me, lying hidden between the potato plants in the Splat one dark night with black cotton tied to his door knocker.

Harold was a master craftsman, and we used to watch him making so many things from cartwheels to complete carts, coffins made so well and with such good quality wood it was a shame to bury them. He also acted as the Undertaker for the village.

I remember one winter's night it was snowing hard. Mother had phoned the County Garage to warn father that the road was impassable but was told he had already left and he was long overdue at home.

She was very worried and asked

Harold and Fred Bale if they would go and find father with a torch and a hot thermos. Now Fred was the Sexton, and when father returned in their company he said to mother "Why did you send the undertaker and gravedigger?"

Fred Bale lived in the lower centre of the village opposite Fairfield with his wife and her sister. Fred was not only the Sexton but also Tower captain of the bell ringers. He was also Quartermaster for the Home Guard and had a shed full of explosive stores and ammunition.

After the war when he had to surrender it all, he was not convinced that there would not be a necessity for some of it in the future to defend Bratton against an unknown invader. He therefore retained a considerable quantity.

When items became time expired he would bury them in his garden, to be found many years later by future occupants of his house. However, when the retained phosphorous grenades started leaking, Fred decided to dispose of the rest of his stores in one go.

He told me that he dug a grave a few feet deeper than usual and buried the lot under some poor soul. Fred said if that lot ever exploded the occupant of the grave would think he had arrived in Hell's fire.

In addition to his other duties Fred Bale was one of the village postmen. He had the round of the outlying farms near Benton. Jack Parkhouse, Pats father had the round towards Challacombe, Alfie Best the round down Loxhore Lane, whilst Fred Muxworthy covered Bratton village.

Bill Dinnicombe lived at Loxhore and had a son John who was our age and visited Bratton to play with us at times. Later they moved to Bratton and lived next door to my married sister. Bill worked for the Council and was responsible for trimming the roadside hedges and clearing the gutters from Loxhore Cross to Ditchends.

There were no tractor driven hedge trimmers in those days, or JCBs. Bill used a sickle or hook to trim the hedges and a brush and spade to clean the gutters. Rain or fine he would be working his way from one end of his beat to the other and the roadsides were in much better shape than they are today. When he finished at one end he would start again at the other.

One day he left his tools by the hedge opposite Harold Parkin's. We boys came out of Laurie's and saw them abandoned there so we hid them behind the hedge. Little did we know Bill was in Harold's workshop having a break and was watching us through the window! He said to Harold, "Look what they young terrors are doing with my tools". We only escaped a cuffing through Bill's good nature.

In later years when Mother and Father were finding it difficult to assist with the washing up after the school party, Bill and his wife would come to help. After Father died I used to attend the party and Bill would always come along for a chat about old times. He always repeated the story of his tools as it tickled him to death.

At the bottom of the village lived Charlie Marshall with his wife Eva and their children Derek and Margaret, later, after they moved to the centre of the village, they had another daughter, Janice. Charlie was a general builder and did many other odd jobs such as chimney sweeping.

A second builder was George Hancock. Between the two they took care of all the villages building needs. In the centre of the village lived Bill and Maud Bale, their son Frank satisfied the village's requirement for a painter together, later, with Laurie's brother.

Along Station Road, by the fork of Button Lane, was Liz Buckle, later joined by her relatives George Carpenter and his son Geoff. Liz was a dressmaker and made most of the clothes for the village.

Another service the village had was that of a resident village policeman. PC Chapman lived in a police house at the bottom of the village, next door to the Lotts, and patrolled his beat pushing his bicycle.

To my knowledge he never had many crimes to solve, the only one I knew of being when an escaped convict from Dartmoor passed through the village and robbed the church poor box. I don't believe he ever had to use his truncheon or handcuffs or even if he carried them.

One winter's day Laurie and I were hiding behind the hedge in Watty Holmes garden, throwing snowballs at unsuspecting passers-by, when PC Chapman came down the road. Laurie dared me, and never being one to funk a dare, I managed the traditional one and knocked his helmet off.

He was not amused and, to our fast retreating rear ends, shouted "I'll take my belt off to you young devils". Truly he did wear a very wide leather belt and we kept well out of his way for some time.

Apart from the snowball incident we never had much to do with him, although we were probably the greatest miscreants in the village. I suppose he ensured, as far as possible, that livestock were not slaughtered for home consumption without a licence.

He also made sure we did not flout the blackout regulations, although the light from our candles and oil lamps would hardly attract the attention of the German bombers, which we frequently heard passing over at night on their way to Cardiff, Swansea and other places.

In fact I believe only one bomb fell on Barnstaple during the whole war and that hit the British Restaurant, but even that may be a fault of my memory.

I suppose nowadays that if a crime was committed at the top of the village, police from Barnstaple would reach the scene in less time than PC Chapman could have got there pushing his bike up the hill, although with today's response times I would not be so sure.

He had few traffic problems, as there were few cars in the village, no speed limits, white or yellow lines, and no stop signs to be flouted. I suppose he might have nabbed Bob Penfold most nights at closing time, as drunk in charge of a horse, but he would not have made himself popular. Anyway the horse was really in charge of Bob.

He did try to get my father one day. We had harvested the crop of cabbages we grew on the Splat and Father had come home for lunch, testing an army lorry on the way. He had the cabbages loaded into it intending to take them to Barnstaple Children's Home on his way back to the County Garage.

PC Chapman saw him, and phoned ahead to Barnstaple police regarding the unauthorised use of an army lorry. Father was stopped in Bear Street but on explaining what he was doing was sent on his way, so PC Chapman did not get a commendation.

I remember on the Police House gate there was a colourful poster describing, and warning about the dangers of, the Colorado Beetle. I think this was the only 'Wanted' poster displayed in Bratton and I don't think PC Chapman ever arrested one of those.

We had our own reservoirs at Castle Moor and Cross Park. At the bottom of the village just over Barn Hill we had our sewerage works for those few houses lucky enough to be on main drainage.

This sewerage works was another playground for us boys. It was normally unattended although supervised by Mr Britton who had a bungalow on Barn Hill. We would peer into the tanks and ride on the rotating spray arms of the filtration plant. Why none of us contracted a terrible disease I shall never know.

We had our own medical service provided by Nurse Moor. She moved into the top of the village from Brayford. I think it was her father, Tommy Moor, who used to deliver our Calor gas bottles from South Molton.

Thus you could say that the village was almost a self sufficient closed community then, being reliant only on Barnstaple for newspapers which were delivered daily by Stan Hill.

Chapter 18

Middle School

Despite my black stars I moved into the intermediate class with the rest of my group. Here, in the middle classroom, our learning started in earnest. I remember our teacher was called 'Fatty' Harris.

She did not use a thin cane like Sam but either a ruler or a heavy beech stick. I remember her being rather annoyed if at the last moment you took your hand back, as Pat did one day, and she hit her own leg.

However, that beech stick really numbed your hand for a long time and made it impossible to hold a pen for the rest of the day.

Her only other failing in our eyes was that she had a rather bad case of B.O. When we had to form a line and follow her around the playground it was a competition to try to get to the rear of the line, but she was a very good teacher.

In this class we graduated to dip pens and ink, with inkwells in the desk. Not only was our work always liberally spattered with ink blotches but so were our fingers, our clothes and everything else.

I seem to remember small pieces of carbide being dropped in the inkwells at times that produced a very satisfying Vesuvius of black bubbles to cover the desk and anyone in the vicinity.

About this time my sister left the school, due to her age, and took a Pitman's Shorthand and Typing course. She then went to work for a solicitor in Barnstaple until she was old enough to join the Wrens as the WRNS was called.

She then also left the village, initially she was stationed at the barracks at Dartmouth. It was there she met Dennis Bye, her husband to be. After the war they lived in the Midlands for some time until their return to Bratton.

We boys were split up in this class and forced to have girls on either side of us, as a calming influence. I sat between two slightly older than myself, Margaret Marshall, Derek's younger sister, and Kathleen Shapland from Stoke Rivers.

I was already very friendly with Margaret and had been from about the age of five. We always danced, or at least circled the floor together, at the Village Hall dances. This friendship persevered until we left Bratton School.

I remember they used to help me to write my capital letters, which I never could remember how to do. My two neighbours soon left to join the top class, we met up later again in the Sam's class, but in the meantime I sat next to Vera Ridd-Jones, who gave me the same assistance.

In the churchyard certain graves were surmounted by glass domes containing china flowers. Under the base of these domes there were nearly always slow worms to be found in the summertime. We boys would gather these reptiles and keep them in our pockets to be placed, at opportune moments, either in the girl's desks or, if possible, slipped into the pockets of their frocks.

When slow worms were not available frogs, toads or lizards made a readily available substitute. Because of these and other misdemeanours, my friends and I still had many meetings with the cane, more frequently now from Fatty than Sam.

On the classroom windowsill we first had a jam jar filled with wet sawdust and lined with a piece of blotting paper, between this and the side we placed a pea. The jar was than wrapped in black paper and we watched the pea germinate. Later we had a tank of frogspawn and watched the tadpoles develop into frogs, after which they escaped into the room, with a little help from us.

I think Fatty must have been a biologist as I clearly remember her killing a frog with chloroform and dissecting it. She pinned it out neatly on a board, as she did it, to show us the heart and lungs etc. probably a very anti-social operation these days. We all found this very interesting and not in the least horrifying.

She also took us for nature rambles which was very brave of her. Mainly our scientific studies consisted of catching frogs for the girl's desks. I remember one time I brought a dead, unusually large, three foot long viper to school, which Bill Bale had killed, this caused quite a sensation in the playground.

On the big cupboard door to our right, was pinned a list of words where 'i before e except after c', did not apply. Over the door was a shelf which held a large wooden box, this was brought down at Christmas and contained dressing up costumes and, what fascinated us most, a large flintlock pistol.

As we approached Christmas Fatty would get us to colour wash a piece of paper and then drop blobs of poster paint on it, holding it vertical caused the paint to run down forming an interesting pattern. We then had to glue this to a piece of card using the 'Gloy' pot and attach a small calendar. These we took home as presents.

In this class we also learned cane work. On Fridays she would produce a large tin bath full of water with lengths of cane soaking in it. The first item we had to make was a glass holder with a round circular ply base, we had to weave cane into a cylinder on it.

After that we graduated to oval trays, with a handle at each end made from coloured beads. They were quite attractive when completed properly, which I never managed to do. We were allowed to take the finished items home. I wonder how many survive today.

I remember one writing task was to copy out a very lengthy serialised story which Miss Harris wrote on the blackboard. As she had chosen an exciting story I quite enjoyed this exercise.

For arithmetic we had to solve sums such as, if a fork costs one shilling and three pence, a spoon one shilling and six pence and a knife two shillings and nine pence, how much would the cutlery for six people cost.

Fatty Harris read us Malcolm Saville's book 'The Mystery at Witchend', about a gang of children in Wales, by the Long Mynd and Stiperstones, who had a camp in a pine wood. They discovered a female German spy.

At this time the Devon County Library service started bringing boxes of books to the school once a fortnight, which we could borrow, and we read all of Malcolm Savilles, 'Seven White Gates' etc. This helped to wean us off the Dandy, Beano and Radio Fun.

We were all still very unaware sexually at this stage, although totally knowledgeable about the act itself for it is impossible not to be in a farming community. All children saw chickens with cockerels, the sheep being put to the ram, the cows being taken to the bull, but it was not until we were about eight we related the behaviour to humans.

I do remember though, an argument developing amongst us, for what reason I do not know, as to whether Fatty wore any knickers.

This argument was settled by a boy who shall be nameless, from 'out over'. Tying a mirror on his shoe he looked up her dress when she was bending over a pupil in front of him. This proved she did wear them and I must say we admired his pluck, as she was a well built woman with quite a temper.

When Fatty was looking at your work

she trapped your head between her arm and ribs and any adverse comment she made was impressed on you by the accompaniment of a sharp slap around the ear.

She fell foul of my mother because of this. Mother had had her ears slapped as a child and suffered a perforated ear drum as a result. After a rather lengthy session of slaps I complained in the evening of a ringing in the ears. My mother paid a visit to the school, after which I appeared to receive more than my share of the cane, but was never again clipped around the ear.

In this class we used the top playground with the two pieces of lawn above. I remember that a German aircraft had crashed somewhere nearby and the older boys had salvaged Perspex from its windshield and used to fashion rings for the girls from it.

We used to sit on the wall beside the playground in break and carve things with the pocket knives that we all carried. You had to have a knife with 'Real Lamb Foot' engraved on the blade to be 'with it'. I believe that on the lawn was a rain gauge and Sam frequently found we had yellow rain, he was not amused.

Whilst in this class the bombing in the

cities slackened, and most evacuees returned to what was left of their homes but continued to visit friends they had made in the village for a considerable time.

Fatty asked the class one day to raise their hands if they had been as far from the village as Barnstaple. About half raised their hands and she then said, "As far as Exeter", and most of the raised hands descended. She then said, "Further than Exeter" and mine was the only hand to stay aloft. Such was the isolation we lived in then.

Despite her strict discipline Fatty was a very good teacher, and we all learnt a great deal during the years we spent in her class. She made all the lessons very interesting. One day Fatty had us all smoking bits of glass in a candle flame and then took us into the playground to watch an eclipse of the sun.

Chapter 19

Toys and Explosives

As most children still do nowadays, we made many of our own toys. We had no help from such TV programmes as Blue Peter, and sticky backed plastic had not been invented then, nor were toilet roll cardboard tubes available, as most houses had to make do with torn up newspaper in the privies.

Paper was very scarce in wartime and the ad lib use of kitchen rolls did not happen until many years later. Our early home made toys were very simple.

Cotton reels were abundant as clothes were always handed down and altered to fit. Candles were also the main form of lighting so were plentiful. Elastic bands were used to bottle jams so our first toys used these three items.

We would cut the raised rims of the cotton reels into serrated edges, cut a half inch length of candle, remove the wick and cut a transverse groove to take a matchstick. On one end of the cotton reel also would be cut a transverse groove and an elastic band would be threaded through the reel and candle, secured at both ends with the matchsticks.

Leaving the stick securing the candle projecting past the rim of the reel the band would be wound up. When placed on a table the band tension would make our 'tank' climb quite steep inclines.

As with all boys our mothers despaired of the loss of our garters for use as catapults, until we graduated to forked twigs and bicycle inner tubes for these.

Similarly they complained of the state of our handkerchiefs which, besides being stained brown with mud, were also torn having been used as parachutes when tied to stones. Long sticks split at the end to accept a stone allowed us to throw stones further than by hand, and with good accuracy.

Long forked sticks with one branch cut short in the form of a sharp cornered J acted as stilts, painful to use in shoes but fine in our hobnail boots. Bows and arrows, swords and spears were made, and used by us, as all boys do.

Green sycamore sticks roughly six inches long had a V cut in about one inch from the end. The green bark was then bruised with the penknife handle until it could be slipped off. A flat was then cut from the V to the near end and the bark replaced forming an effective whistle.

Two pieces of slate held astride the index fingers made good clappers. With these and the whistles, together with Laurie's Jew's harp and Buster's mouth organ, we had a band. I never got on with the Jew's harp and usually cut my lip or gave myself toothache.

A popgun could be made by sticking a cut off bicycle spoke in a piece of ash twig and wrapping the other end with wool to form a seal that fitted inside an elder twig, from which the pith had been removed. This contrivance would fire a piece of chewed newspaper a considerable distance.

Laurie's brother used to make the most realistic models of aircraft of the time, even four engine bombers. These were works of art and carved out of solid wood.

I was horrified one day, after he had taken one to school, to see him being chased by older boys who took one of these models from him and threw it in the air to see if it would fly. Of course it would not, and merely crashed into the road and broke into smithereens. I was devastated at its destruction, I think even more than George, who was very philosophical.

From these innocent beginnings we graduated to far more dangerous pastimes.

The first unfortunate episode I remember concerned my mother's pistol. She had visited France during the First World War and had acquired a .38 revolver and a quantity of ammunition. I came across this one day and purloined one of the bullets.

We took it out into the wash house at Craigside, balanced the percussion cap on a pebble and Buster hit it with a hammer. In the ensuing explosion a piece of the brass casing penetrated his boot but very fortunately no other injury was caused.

Hearing the bang mother came flying out of the house and, perceiving what had happened, chastised me more than somewhat. She also gave the revolver and remaining ammunition to father for instant disposal.

Our future explosions were confined to our own efforts. Hollow door keys were filled with the heads of red top matches, tied to a string and a blunt nail secured to the other end. The nail being inserted in the key and the whole contrivance swung against a wall. If the key survived the ensuing explosion it could be reused. Laurie had the impudence to perform this operation one day just behind his father and was rewarded with a sound cuffing.

Carbide was our favourite source of

explosive. It was in common use in those days for acetylene lamps but is probably unobtainable now so I will not be endangering young lives by an explanation of our usage.

Carbide bombs were of two types, bottle and can. The bottle type was a spring top pop bottle, with a piece of carbide inside and a drop of water on it. As the gas that formed expanded so the bottle exploded. Insufficient water meant insufficient pressure of gas and no explosion.

I remember one that did not go off being retrieved by Ginger Squires, Ronnie's younger brother. As he picked it up it did go off, quite gently fortunately but covering him with a white gooey mess of dissolved carbide although causing no other injury. He survived unharmed, apart from his clothes, but was killed at Snapper in a motorcycle accident many years later.

The can type was our favourite. An empty treacle tin would have a nail hole punched in the base. The carbide would be inserted and wetted and the tin lid stamped on tight. With a match stuck in the end of a long stick the gas air mixture issuing from the hole would be ignited and the tin would disappear in one direction and the lid in the opposite, accompanied by a loud explosion. This type was carried to its ultimate form by Laurie's brother George in the cricket field.

He used a five gallon oil drum, a large quantity of carbide and a long newspaper fuse. The drum exploded, ascending about fifty feet in the air and every window in Bratton rattled. I trust George will forgive me for letting this little secret out, as he swore everyone to secrecy for fear of recriminations. As we are all in our seventies now I think we are safe from chastisement by our elders.

There were many flies around in the houses during the summer, possibly attracted by the unhygienic methods of farming and the proximity of many dung heaps and earth closets. Most houses had fly papers hanging in each room and used Flit guns regularly. Another remedy appeared in the shops consisting of a small steel cylinder with a brass frangible seal filled with pressurised DDT gas.

The method of their use was to break the seal and leave the cylinder in a closed room for about ten minutes, after which you ventilated the room and swept up the corpses. We found that these unopened cylinders when rolled up in newspaper which was then set alight, exploded with a very satisfying noise.

At one time the Home Guard carried out an exercise, hiding packets of blank .303 rifle ammunition in the hedgerows to simulate anti-personnel bombs dropped by German aircraft. Their exercise was to locate and retrieve all of these 'bombs'.

However whenever the Home Guard had any exercise we boys were always in attendance to see the fun. We used to exasperate the members by pointing out their camouflaged positions to the 'enemy' and such other amusing tricks. On this particular exercise we spirited away many packets of these blank cartridges. These again wrapped in burning newspaper produced an exciting noise.

All of the above activities now seem completely idiotic when viewed from our senile age. We would all be absolutely horrified if we felt that any of our children or grandchildren indulged in such activities.

We would probably call the police, but certainly inform the parents, if we saw any child behaving in this way now. It must be by the grace of God that not a single one of us ever sustained the slightest injury from any of these stupid pranks.

We boys were not alone in misusing explosives and our elders should have known better, but this was not always the case as the following episode testifies. Fred Ewens and Bill Merrett kept bees, in their gardens but at certain times moved them up to the field above cricket field. They had a barbed wire fence there to keep the sheep away from the hives, and one year found the wooden posts were rotten.

They obtained new posts and laid them beside the fence awaiting an opportunity to put them up. They noticed on the next visit that some of the posts were missing and Fred Ewens decided to find out where they were going.

He took a post home and drilled a hole in one end, filled it with explosive, plugged it and replaced the post with the rest. A short time later there was a very loud explosion in somebody's house, and the top of the Rayburn was destroyed. Fortunately nobody was hurt.

The lady of the house concerned was in Bill Merrett's shop shortly after the event, and Bill said he had heard about the bang, and that you could not rely on what you might find in the coal these days. The lady did not believe his innocence and reckoned he knew something about it, but of course was unable to expand on her theory. All very amusing but potentially disastrous.

Chapter 20

The Village Hall

By an Indenture of 1841 the land for the erection of School Rooms and Masters house was ceded by the then Rector, one Humphrey Senhouse Pinder. When the new school was built as a Devon County Council school in 1906 the old buildings were occasionally used as overflow school accommodation.

Village Hall minus Front Garden

At other times it was employed as the Village Hall, and the Master's house was used for the caretaker. It was purchased by the village as a result of Public Subscription in 1963. Not much used before the outbreak of war it became indispensable during the

1940s.

Soon after we arrived in Bratton it was looked after by Mrs Mitchell who moved, with her husband and daughter Stella, into the attached house.

Half way down the Hall was a side room for coats and at the far end just by the stage a door led off to another room in which was a large table, used for setting out refreshments and the tea urn. These refreshments were carried out to the Hall at functions on large tin trays, by volunteers.

From this room a door to Mrs Mitchell's living accommodation led into her kitchen where she boiled the water for the tea on her range. Most evenings when the Hall was in use Gandhi could be seen asleep in front of the range.

The Hall itself could accommodate the whole population then. It was lit by large oil lamps suspended from the ceiling on chains. A skittle alley ran down the side nearest the road, the balls being stopped by half car tyres nailed to the wall. On function nights the alley would be leant up against the wall.

There were two ventilators in the ceiling which were surmounted by rain shields but they did not provide enough ventilation when the energetic farmers were sweating their way through a dance, so even in winter the door and windows were normally cracked open. Halfway down the room was a concertina wooden partition, which came into use when the school was overcrowded, enabling two extra classrooms to be provided in the Hall.

On the wall hung a picture of the current Vicar, Philip Cave-Moyle. I cannot remember much about him except his wife chased us out of Rectory grounds a few times. However, I believe we went in fear and trembling of him, probably due to the fact that we once put buttons in the Sunday school collection, and kept the money for sweets or cigarettes.

Father and Mother, together with other villagers, formed the Whist Drive Committee which held its inaugural meeting in the front room at Craigside. The whist drives, held in the Hall proved very popular and continued until the 1980s.

On whist drive nights I was either sent to stay overnight at Pat's or at Maud Bale's. I much preferred Pat's where we spent most of the night talking in the double bed. However, at Maud's I used to be kept quiet by being given a bottle of Tivvy, the local beer, by Frank who babysat for me. I used to drink it feeling very grown up sitting on the table whilst he played darts in the living room with his friends.

It was he, on one of these nights, who discussed the fact with his friends that if you removed the shot from a twelve bore cartridge and substituted a candle, it would penetrate an oak door. This gave me ideas that I was to exploit later.

My father did not serve on the Whist Drive Committee for long as he objected to playing cards with children. Babysitters were scarce so people would bring their children, as young as nine, with them and teach them to play. Village whist drives were not social affairs but vicious competitions.

If someone had a poor hand and an opponent laid a wrong card by mistake the shout would go up "Revoke, nine four" and they claimed the hand. Also tempers would fray at a 'Progressive' drive if the partner did not reply to a small value led card by putting on their highest.

Although the prizes were small the villagers were very competitive and Father always felt so sorry for youngsters who incurred the wrath of their elders, over a simple mistake, that he refused to play any longer.

Soon after arriving in the village my mother became friendly with an evacuee, Mrs Sugden. She had a teenage daughter Rosemary and lived down Button, where Miss Fanshawe lived, until moving to the bottom of the village. Mrs Sugden and Mother started the local branch of the Women's Institute, which met in the Hall and was a great success.

Mother also started the concerts, I think I was rather unpopular then, as all my friends got roped in to act in them. I had to say poetry as well as act, and mother had us rehearsing for hours.

I remember one piece that I had to recite called "The man who does the garden", which everyone associated with Bert Antel who did ours. One line was, "It's terrible the waste of soap in other people's houses, the proper way to wash your hands is rub 'em down your trousers". This caused great merriment among the audience of which Bert was a member.

Of the sketches I can only remember, "A penny for the Guy", with all four of us boys in it, and Laurie made up as the Guy in an old wheelbarrow, but I can't remember the words. There was also one which I performed with my sister when I only had to keep saying "Why?" much to her assumed exasperation. I think this mirrored our real life situation.

I also remember one sketch which my mother performed with Maud Bale. During it they were meant to be having an argument whilst Mother was baking. Unrehearsed, during this scene, Mother ad-libbed and threw some dough at Maud, a very surprised Maud retaliated and the audience was in stitches while a battle of flying dough took place on the stage, as both ladies were known to have fierce tempers.

We had many dances and socials in the Hall. As nearly all the village attended these entertainments there was nobody to baby-sit so we children attended most functions. We would to sit on the edge of the stage by the band and put rude words to most of the songs, especially 'Neath the shade of the old apple tree' and the one they always played at the end 'After the ball was over'.

I think we had 'The Squadronaires' and the 'Three R's' bands mostly. The dances were fund raising events for 'The Spitfire Fund' or 'Battleship Fund'. The Hall used to be crowded and the older boys commandeered the small table at the back as a seat, next to old Charlie Clarke who took the money. In later years when we were older we went back there and took their place at functions, and square dances when these were started.

We also had the school Christmas parties in the Hall, with a conjuror or Punch and Judy, followed by a film show and games. We used the cloakroom half way down the side of the Hall as the room you went to receive a letter or parcel in 'Postman's Knock'. Apart from that and 'Musical Chairs' and 'Pass the Parcel' I cannot remember the games.

The skittle alley would be stood against the wall and an extension to the stage put across the gap for the concert productions. A curtain was erected and the refreshment room used as a changing room. Mrs Mitchell would be heating great kettles of water on the Bodley for the teas at refreshment time.

I remember at one rehearsal we four boys were running around the Hall chasing each other and jumping on and off a table on each circuit, just as I was jumping off Rachel Champion put out her arm to stop me and I went flat on my face and broke my nose. It's never been the same since.

During the war we used to have government propaganda film shows held in the Hall, the projectionist came out from Barnstaple, and the Hall was so crowded we often had to sit on the floor. I remember some of the propaganda shorts that he showed, 'The

Squander Bug', a fat little devil with a forked tail, covered in swastikas, which sat on your shoulder and persuaded you to spend your money rather than invest in National Savings.

I remember another on the theme of 'Coughs and sneezes spread diseases, trap them in your handkerchieves', a man sneezed in a restaurant and all the droplets turned into little German parachutists who descended on people, and their food, and started climbing up their noses with fixed bayonets. So propaganda did make some impression after all, even Chad looking over the wall with his 'Wot No ----?'. There were also the cartoons, especially liked was Popeye.

Do they still put soap flakes on the floor before a dance I wonder? One use to which the roof ventilators were put was to disrupt functions, by the youth of the village.

It was John Bowden and John Dinnicombe who sat on the roof, lifted off the ventilator lid, and poured a bucket of water down on the Dancing Class. Evidently when the ventilator was lifted off a shower of dust and rust descended. This caused all the occupants to look up so they received the water full in the face.

Whilst Pat and Laurie, who had encouraged them, rolled around laughing hidden in the Churchyard, Charlie Ward, the then Chairman of the Village Hall Committee, chased the other two into the night but never caught them, luckily for them, as severe retribution was promised if he ever found the perpetrators.

Much later my sister Beryl and her husband Dennis Bye, who had come to live in the village at Sunshine Cottage, started the Old Time Dancing committee. It was just getting off the ground when Marshall Challis, the evangelist, came to the village with his tent and converted them. They immediately resigned from the committee as they then considered dancing to be the Devils work.

Beryl persuaded all us boys to go to a revivalist meeting in the Hall and at the end the audience were asked to put their hand up if they were saved. We all sat on ours but various people went up to be saved.

I think it was the worst hour or two we ever spent but as we had been sat in the front row we could not make our escape. I know that Beryl's conversion to religion was to cause my poor mother much unnecessary anguish late in her life, and much trouble for both my parents.

Mother discovered the game of Beetle and organised 'Beetle Drives'. You threw dice in turn for body, head, legs and feelers, and grabbed the dice from each other to throw and the first one to complete the drawing shouted out 'BEETLE'. These were always well attended and great fun for young and old. I presume they have now been replaced by Bingo.

There were no Public toilets in the village, and whereas this did not bother us if we were out in the countryside, when were playing near the Hall we would avail ourselves of the toilet block. If spotted we were unceremoniously chased out by Mrs Mitchell who had the responsibility of cleaning it.

In 1944 the dances were also attended by some of the GIs camping in the area prior to D day. This was not appreciated by the local lads who stood little chance with the village maidens when these tall, lean, uniformed Yanks appeared, their pockets full of nylons and candy.

The following are some of the favourite songs of the time sung at community sing songs in the Hall:-

'She'll be coming round the mountains when she comes'
'Silver wings in the moonlight'

'Deep in the heart of Texas'
'Johnny got a Zero, got another Zero today'
'Coming in on a wing and a prayer'
'All the nice girls love a sailor'
'Chocolate soldier from the USA'
'Look for the silver lining'
'We're going to hang out the washing'
'You are my sunshine'
'I've got sixpence'
'Run rabbit run'
'Lily of Laguna'
'Twas on the Isle of Capri'

There was a great spirit of camaraderie during the war and the Village Hall helped to foster it to a great extent. Any war is a terrible thing, and the type of wars conducted these days do not engender the same feeling among the general public, as did the Second World War, which affected everyone in some way. It is hard to describe the emotions of the time, when so many loved ones were engaged in battle overseas or living through the terrible bombing in the cities, but in some ways many considered that those were the happiest days of their lives.

I think, as far as we boys were concerned we just hoped that it would not finish before we had a chance to join up. I am sure we were extremely lucky that it did end otherwise most of us would probably not be here today.

I know, in 1945 my only ambition was to join my brother in the RAF but it was to be another seven years before the RAF would train me to fly.

Chapter 21

The Triangle

The roads from Sentry Cross to Ditchends and Four Cross Way back to the village were known as the Triangle and were frequently walked by our families on a Sunday.

By Sentry Cross there was a sloping field on the right, down which we used to sledge in the winter, whether it was on snow, or whether there was a spring forming an ice slide, I cannot remember. We would walk to the right at the Cross, along the flat, until the slight climb as we pass Dallyn's farm.

Further on, just inside the field on the left, are the humps and bumps of old iron mine workings. To the right is a massive concrete structure covered in ivy. On this at one time was mounted the engine that hauled up the ore from the iron mines down in the cleave at Haxton Down, Ern Britton's farm. The mines ceased operations in the 19th. Century and the entrances were sealed.

We four boys used to take a storm lantern and climb down to the mine entrances. To my recollection there were three shafts whose entrances had been blocked by soil and had become totally obscured by undergrowth.

However due to settlement there were gaps at the top of the blockages about the size of a badgers hole. One of the shafts was completely filled with water but the other two were accessible if you squeezed through the hole and slid down the slopes inside to the shaft floor.

One was extremely long and narrow and we explored it to the end, it ran straight back into the hillside under the road. The second went in a short way before it expanded into a large chamber with three passages leading off. After a short distance, however, all three were blocked with roof falls.

We went there many times and searched for other entrances as well, but only found the three. If anything had happened to trap us in there we would never have been found for nobody had any idea we went there. If they had known we would have been forbidden in this, as in many of our other escapades. The danger we were in horrifies me today and I hope that these mine workings are now completely sealed.

In fact this area of North Devon is very rich in mineral deposits. I have visited the mine workings at Charles near East Buckland, the coal mines at North Molton and the Silver mine at Coombe Martin. I have also heard that according to legend small amounts of gold were mined on Exmoor.

At the bottom of the valley by the stream was a water ram, pumping up water to the Haxton Down farm house, which we examined closely. We could not puzzle out how it worked continuously without apparent power and it was not until many years later in science classes that I found out.

In later years I was given permission by Ern Britton to shoot rabbits all over the cleave and spent many happy hours there stalking them, but that was before myxomatosis.

Back on the road a slight downhill to Benton lane. At the top of the lane on the small grass triangle stood a wooden privy. Why it was placed there far away from any house was a mystery. I only know that someone used it one day, only to notice, having completed his business that, instead of the bucket, carefully folded inside the bucket area was the greatcoat belonging to a man who worked at Benton!

Further along the road, as you approach Ditchends, on the left grow tall

Beech trees, home to both carrion crow and ordinary crows. I seem to remember that the carrion's eggs are almost sea green covered in small brown spots, whilst the ordinary crow's eggs are sky blue with large black spots. Their nests were the reason for many trips to this area. At Ditchends there is a triangle of tall fir trees housing a rookery, some more of the few trees we could not climb.

As you round the corner to the left, on the right is the Brayford automatic telephone exchange, also a telephone box but why it is there, so far from habitation, we never knew. Just along the road that way is the junction of the roads to Brayford, East Buckland and Stoke Rivers.

It was here my father had one of his few car accidents. He was canvassing for the first elections after the war for the Liberal candidate, Jeremy Thorpe. His car was covered with stickers and on the corner he bumped into the Conservative candidate canvasser's car. Was it deliberate? Father said not.

Continuing left towards Four Cross Way are tall hedges of Beech with many nests, there being nobody around to disturb the occupants, most of these crow's nests we plundered from time to time. Then inside a gate on the left is a series of humps. This was presumed to be an old Roman encampment, of which there are also two or three along the East Buckland road.

In the centre of the camp there is a pond, a rather dirty smelly, cow hole of a pond but the only stretch of still water near Bratton so it was to here we carried a RAF dinghy which I had acquired, inflated it, raised the sail and set off. Not a terribly enjoyable experience but still it floated.

Further along, past Bert Heal's Cape Farm on the right, now the home of Exmoor Steam Railway, is Four Cross Way. To the right are the hump back bridges on the road to Challacombe. In 1944 Rex came home on leave and he had bought a three wheel Morgan sports car.

He gave me one of the most memorable rides of my life along this road. The Morgan, going flat out, left the ground over each hump back bridge to the accompaniment of whoops of joy from its young passenger. It was amazing that the road builders would go to the expense of building these bridges as cattle passages from one side of the road to the other on such a little used road.

The road continues straight ahead to Friendship where there are two large brick cylinders in the field on the right, whose purpose we could not discover. Further along is Blackmoor Gate where we once cycled to try to reclaim money on three old AA badges we had found. The AA man said they no longer gave back five shillings on each but kept the badges and thanked us. I reckon he kept the fifteen shillings too.

Laurie and I also cycled out here in later years to see where a Vampire aircraft from Chivenor had crashed. I seem to remember we found and retrieved one of its cannons. However we could not straighten the bent barrel enough to get it to fire twelve bore cartridges, as we had hoped.

Going left it is flat to the top of Grange Hill. In a field on the left here, there is a smaller but cleaner and deeper pond. Here we saw a kingfisher for the first time and also found on the bank a small twig of furze covered in fleas. I think it was Laurie who explained, or someone later that told us, it was possibly a fox de-fleaing itself.

We were told that the fox would hold the furze stick in its mouth, wade into the stream swim across and stay submerged except for its nose. All its fleas would climb onto the stick which it would carefully place on the bank before swimming off and emerging elsewhere. Is it true? There was certainly a flea covered stick with no other logical explanation.

Rosemarie Ewens, Eva Webber and Laurie's Mum
On Grange Hill.

Going down Grange Hill, we could look right over Bratton to Barnstaple Bay and Hartland point. My brother Rex flew low over here piloting a bomber, on a training exercise, during the war in 1944 and gave the height as 800ft.

It was to be another eight years before I would pilot a Tiger Moth from Exeter with

Laurie on board over the same countryside, waving to his brother George in the road below. Laurie said he had never been so cold in his life as in the open cockpit of that biplane.

It was from here that we would start our bicycle races, never touching the pedals or brakes until we had passed through the village and were at the top of Barn Hill. On the right was the start of the pleasure ground. Nothing was ever done to improve the field and certainly nobody ever used it. Now, I understand, it is being used for buildings housing small businesses.

A little further down the main road was the old village pump on the left hand side. It was in a small stone chamber down some steps and was still working when we first knew it. When Fred Ewens was a boy he used to put a handful of sand in the pump which stopped it working and deprived the top of the village of their water supply. I think if he had been younger he would have qualified for our gang.

This pump was also used as a position for one of the three Bus Stops in the village, the others being at the White Hart and Cart Linhay. However the bus normally stopped for you anywhere you wished.

Just below, on the right, is Belle Vue and the three attached cottages, all of which my parents bought in 1946 when we moved to the central cottage 'Moorland View'. We later moved again into the first cottage, named 'The Cottage', as it had a bathroom. My parents lived there until their deaths. We had bought the whole row from Arthur Bowden who lived behind Belle Vue but we sold Belle Vue back to his son, Jack, who with his wife Nancy and their three children, John, Janet and Michael, lived in the front.

Belle Vue and Cottages

Later Father also bought the field

behind, which became the subject of a Compulsory Purchase order for the building of the council houses, but he ensured that the service road for them would be routed along the rear of the existing houses. He also bought the building plot in the field opposite The Cottage to maintain the view to Stoke Rivers. He later sold this plot on the understanding that it would be used for a road and never be built on.

Chapter 22

Button River

Another favourite Sunday walk with our parents was down to Button River and along to the Mill. We would start by the White Hart, where there was a little triangle of grass on which we often played and called the 'Village Green'. Fred Ewens let off a great flare from the Home Guard stores on the Green to celebrate VE night on 8th May.

This was our only enjoyment that day that I remember, whilst our elders had a party in the pub. We did have a celebration on the next day when my father organised a sports day on the Cricket Field, and the Parish Council provided a tea in the Village Hall. On VJ night though, we had a huge bonfire and fireworks at Sentry Cross.

Along Station Road on the right was the back window of the snug bar of the White Hart. This was always open in summer to let the smoke out and was where we used to talk to our elders and occasionally get a glass of cider passed to us. We could just see the dartboard on the right hand wall.

Just past here was the back door to the pub yard inside of which there were buckets full of beer bottle tops, we adorned our shirts with Starkey, Knight and Ford metal tops supported by the cork washers on the inside.

At the first cottage on the left lived Mr Norman who cut our hair. We knelt on a chair whilst he used clippers so blunt that we swore he just entangled them in our hair and pulled it out by the roots. Pat refused to go a second time and we all ended up going to Edwards, the barber in Joy Street, after the Saturday film show.

In the second cottage, at one time owned by my parents, lived an evacuee from the London bombing, 'Snag' Walton and his son, they had no furniture and ate their meals off an upturned tea chest covered in newspaper.

He had the longest blackest nails ever seen, which was why Pat christened him Snag. I suffered a few scratches from them as he just missed catching hold of me one day after we had been ragging him.

Along Station road was the wide area in front of the Village Hall. Here we played pitch and toss against the church wall. We watched the stonemason carve the memorial to Basil Fanshawe in the gatepost. We sat for hours on the iron railings in front of the war memorial. We climbed into the Yew tree by the gate and collected the sticky Yew berries.

We caught the ever present Slow Worms under the glass flower domes on the graves just inside, and from the rose bushes in front of the Village Hall we collected Hips to get the hairy seeds we called "Itchy coos" which we put down each others necks. Here too we played rounders using the pillars and gateposts as "homes".

A little further on there was a hole in the school hedge from where you could ring the school bell with a well aimed air rifle shot, disappearing rapidly before Sam Bentham appeared from his house.

The school house, beside the school, had a delicious pear tree in its back garden. For scrumping those pears and for throwing the firework in his front garden all four of us got a taste of Sam's cane. Next on the right was the gate to the field that ran behind the school. My father rented that field to graze our sheep.

In the field on the left stood two large water cisterns serving Holywell, whether fed from springs or from Castle Moor reservoir I do not know. Just before the fork in the road was Bragan House, (Bracken in our time), where Mary Tame lived, her father Jim was a solicitors clerk in Barnstaple. There was also a girl called Pat Smith living there but whether she was a relative or evacuee I cannot remember.

At the rear door of their house were very large round weights suspended on steel wires. When wound up by hand during the day they would slowly descend at night operating a petrol gas generator to provide gas light to the house. A little further on was Liz Buckle's house

Taking the left fork there was a low Beech hedge on the left, there were also occasional tall Beech trees to carve our initials on, whilst the tall hedge on the right was the only source we knew of lizards.

Normally when we caught them their tails dropped off and wriggled away, until sundown we understood. A clump of trees on the left then marked the entrance drive to Holywell, where Basil and later his son Captain Fanshawe lived.

On the other side of the entrance grew the Monkey Puzzle tree, about the only tree for miles we did not climb, apart from the tall firs. We kept out of Holywell grounds mostly, for fear of Alfie Lavercombe and his shot gun, but we did get over the hedge here and raid the orchard one evening in a very strong party with some girls.

Alfie came after us and we beat a hasty retreat down to the river, Ivy Sage slipped and fell into a bed of stinging nettles in the chase. I was behind her and was gallant enough to stop and help her up.

Down the hill was the quarry on the right where grew a bank of reeds. These were hollowed out for pea shooters and also to make pop guns with a bicycle spoke wound with wool.

As well as there being a garage in the quarry there was another on the other side of the road with a concrete hard standing in front of it. I remember us sitting there whilst someone, I think it was Geoff Carpenter, showed us how to make whistles out of sycamore twigs with our penknives.

Just below was Quarry House on the left, inhabited by a Captain Maynard. He tried to start the scouts but unfortunately the date chosen to start clashed with Loxhore fête and Captain Maynard would not change the date.

We, therefore, did not turn up and so Scouts were never started. However we used to spy on the Girl Guides, which he did start, on the tennis courts below and drop stones onto their tents.

A bit further on the left was the back entrance to the Station with an iron notice board proclaiming it to be 'Railway Property'. Further down, before Bratton Station, was the bridge where we always walked along the parapet and then the Station entrance. Just inside on the left was a bank where lovely wild strawberries grew, nothing tastes quite like them. Under the bridge hung white lime stalactites.

We would take the left fork then, to Button Bridge, here on the right was a broad grass verge where grew many Hazelnut trees. Raymond Bennett's father often came this far and would pull nut laden branches down for us with his white stick. How he saw them when he was blind did not puzzle us unduly.

On the bridge, we would play Pooh sticks. Set into the bridge parapet was a slate with a line down, engraved Loxhore one side and Bratton the other, marking the parish boundaries. Over the bridge to the right was Rye Park, Wallace Heals land, he was nicknamed Timothy Treaclebum by Laurie for some reason. Straight on went to Smythapark, Comer Clarke's farm.

We would walk left through the gate along the footpath, into the meadow where in spring the slope is covered in primroses. I always thought of that as Primrose Hill.

Button Bridge

On the lower slopes also grew massive, tall, thistles which, when we were very young, we would spend a long time felling with our pen knives. Along to the left it was a little marshy, and rushes and Kingcups grew, but over the river hedge was our island.

We called it Pear Drop Island, due to its shape, with deep water one side and shallows the other. Here we built shelters, lit fires, climbed the trees, made rope bridges, caught fish, and generally enjoyed ourselves on many occasions.

A little further on a gate led into the wood. On the left a small offshoot of the river held many minnows, very difficult to catch.

On the far bank was Bluebell Wood, an absolute picture in the flowering season, a complete carpet of blue under the fir trees.

Out of the wood and across the water meadow, on the far side of which we once saw a Stag watching us from the wood. Over the wooden bridge to the mill. I seem to remember in the early days that the wheel still turned and the mill was worked, but it soon became derelict.

There was a friendly family called Tamlyn living in the mill house, (which used to get flooded regularly), but later there was a rather cantankerous person called Goschalk. He had a fierce dog that, when we were walking past one day, bit Laurie on the elbow. This caused me to load the shotgun I was carrying, and threaten to shoot the dog if he did not call it off.

Fred Bale used to get set upon by this dog when he delivered the mail, and despite his complaints it was never kept under control, so that one day he carried a large stick. As the dog sprang out of the hedge at him he laid about it. The dog avoided him after that, but we wished he had taken his stick to the owner instead

Out of the farmyard we would walk up Loxhore Lane. Past the blown up bridge, to the orchard entrance by the old barn on the right. The first tree inside had fallen down, but continued to grow horizontally, and bore lovely crisp sweet apples.

It was further down in the orchard by the railway line that Art Heal caught me up a tree with my shirt stuffed with apples for Laurie and myself. When asked what I was doing I said we had been playing on the line with a ball and it had lodged in the tree. He said that by the look of my shirt I had now retrieved it and I'd better come down.

I think it was another occasion, which Laurie well remembers, in the same orchard. I was up the tree again throwing apples down to Laurie who was putting them in two piles saying, "One for you" and "One for me", when an unseen Art piped up with "How about one for me", we scarpered quick that time.

However he was one of our more friendly farmers and would always allow us to ride up the village on the back of his cart.

Next on the right was a field with a quarry, used as a dump, which included many fascinating items, an old motorcycle frame which we wondered if we could rebuild, and some parts of an old suit of armour. So on past Pennyall Farm which locals referred to as 'Pennyhole' and up to the top of the lane. The house on the right hand corner was the home of Gerald Ley, about our age.

There was usually a circular saw working in the barn here cutting logs, but we did not tarry if not with our parents, as we were on enemy territory and, if caught by Raymond or Gordon Lott or Derek Marshall, the lower village gang, we were in for a hiding. We were not safe until we passed Fairfield gate.

Past the water cistern on the right and Bill Bales on the left, if by ourselves we might run a little in case Maude came out. She did not like young boys hanging around her house. Rachel Champion's and Ivy Sage's houses were on the right. Ivy's sister Mary unfortunately died of diphtheria in 1941.

On the left, outside the entrance to Watty's and Dickie's drive, was another slate water cistern. It was from here that Laurie's family obtained all their water as, in common with many houses, they were not connected to the mains at that time.

Chapter 23

Haxton Lane

Yet another Sunday walk was through the Haxtons, starting beside Lower shop. This shop was where we used to buy our pop, Corona in large bottles with wire caged stoppers, if we could afford it, or smaller snap cap bottles if we were hard up. Sometimes we would get refunds of a penny each on empty jam jars we collected to fund our purchases.

I remember the first oranges and bananas arriving there at the end of the war which we bought against the coupons from the back of our ration books. We also bought saccharine tablets, when we could not get sweets, and licked them. I've hated saccharine ever since.

Round the corner into Haxton Lane, on the right there was a wooden milk churn stand where the Huxtables and Pooks of Haxton used to leave their churns for collection. This was a favourite seat for us whilst planning excursions or devilment.

At the entrance to Rectory Drive there was an open area. Here we used to tie four pieces of string to the corners of our handkerchiefs and with a stone underneath see who could get their parachute highest. Just inside the Drive, in the early days of the war, was an abandoned car in which we used to play.

Around the first bend in the Drive there was always a magpie's nest that we used to raid. The tall fir trees in the entrance were about the only trees we could not climb, our early air rifles would not reach up to the rooks to do any damage but later with more powerful ones we spent one day decimating them.

There was living opposite, Cyrus Parkin, who Laurie said rather liked rook pie so we dumped our haul over his back gate. There were so many corpses that on his return he could not open the gate!

Down the lane, unpaved of course, the first gate on the left led into a field that had a stream running through a marshy area. In winter this would freeze over and it was one of the places we used to go sledging. Sometimes down the lane we would come across Bill Bale and friends, ferreting.

I remember one day their ferret had lain up and they had sent down a line ferret after it, as it would not come up to the smell of guts staked outside of the hole. We watched them having to dig out both ferrets. I think it was also here that one man shot at a rabbit on top of the hedge and hit another man on the other side in the head, luckily not doing him serious damage.

As the lane slopes steeply here and the banks are so high there had in the past been a slip of part of the left hedge leaving a sparsely vegetated area. Here was the best place to dig for underground nuts. You dug with your penknife carefully down the root of the plant, a very thin thread, until you reached the misshapen tuber. This when peeled was crunchy with a slightly peppery taste.

Here also grew sour-sabs, although they were fairly universal as was the plant called Bread and Cheese, the leaves tasting of cheese and the flowers forming the bread. These together with young Beech leaves formed our between meal snacks.

At the bottom of the lane, on the right was the entrance to the field called Buttle or Buddle, with a large stream at the bottom and two smaller streams running parallel along the hillside. These streams were a constant source of enjoyment for us, they were full of frogs and patches of frog spawn, toads and strings of toad spawn.

We caught innumerable frogs here and

spent many hours constructing dams with clats and building other waterworks. I seem to remember also that it was in Buttle that we first tried smoking dried grass rolled up in paper. A little further down the lane, and round the right hand bend was where we used to explode our tin carbide bombs.

Next on the right, but a field away from the lane is Pit Field. Here the streams from Buttle combined to form a small river. Half way down the field it went over a small waterfall forming a deep (to us then) pool. Below the pool there were many 'Dumpheads' living. I later came to believe that these were the same fish referred to in "Lorna Doone" as Miller's Thumb.

The best way to catch these was with a dining fork, we waded barefoot in the stream turning over each flat stone carefully. If you were careful enough, and there was a Dumphead there, it would pause a moment before flashing off upstream to find a new hiding place. The pause was just long enough to impale it with your fork.

In the centre of Pit Field there was an oval ring of trees where presumably in the past there had been a cottage, but all signs of that had long vanished. We used to retreat here with our catch and light a fire against the shelter of a tree trunk cooking them on it in old tins, with a little water.

In the ring of trees there was one wild plum tree which produced rather sour plums. At the top of the field there were some tall ash trees that usually had crows nesting in them from where we would supplement our egg collections, taking them down to our camp and blowing them.

Haxton Lane

Back in Haxton Lane it was a pull up to the top of the hill, a short flat, and then we would turn left at the cross roads where the other roads led to the three farms making up the small hamlet of Haxton. These housed the Huxtable, Squire and Pook families at the time. Michael Huxtable, Raymond (or Ginger) Squire and Beryl Pook were at school with us.

George Pook, Beryl's father, later gave me permission to shoot over all his land. The left hand fork led towards Haxton Down, but we would turn left again by Higher Haxton cottage also owned by the Huxtables.

In those days the cottage was derelict, and a Barn owl used to nest in the northern bedroom. Later a Polish gentleman, Mr. Karneivicz a jobbing builder, lived there after he had renovated it. He also built my fathers garage at The Cottage, and from him I bought my powerful BSA air rifle.

From there we would work our way back across the fields towards the Rectory. I remember one day both Laurie and I were carrying air rifles. I climbed over a gate and, as Laurie was having difficulty getting over with his gun, I said "Here let me take it", and pulled it towards me by the end of the barrel.

What I had not realised was that he had no trigger guard and as the trigger contacted the top bar of the gate it went off. The pellet entered my cheek and travelled up to my cheek bone and lodged there, and there it remains to this day. It shows up every time the dentist X-rays that side of my mouth and at times I can feel it prominent in my cheek.

The footpath in those days ran through the front yard of Rectory Cottages. You had to go down the long flight of stone steps beside the end cottage and pass through the courtyard in front of them.

Shortly after the cottages you cross over the culvert where a small child, an evacuee I think, by the name of Frampton, was drowned. He and his little sister were playing in the stream when he was swept into the culvert.

Men searched all evening to try to find him and it was only when the little girl said "He went swimming" that they thought to look under the culvert, find and rescue him, but too late. I remember it well, as my father joined the search party and we sat at home waiting to hear the outcome. It was very sad.

The path led into Rectory Drive, bordered by rhododendrons, at the top a white gate led into Rectory Lane. On the right just before the gate were many tall fir trees forming a wood in the triangle between Rectory Drive and the lane to Rectory Farm. Here we used to hunt very frequently in the dense undergrowth. Here also nested more rooks.

Later from my bedroom window in Moorland View it used to be a long shot with an air rifle, over an open field, before the houses were built, to send a pellet rattling amongst the tree tops frightening the rooks into flight.

At Rectory Farm the mill was still in working order and we often watched the water wheel turning. I think they used it mainly to drive a circular saw. It was farmed by Mr Snell. There was a pond in the field above and the overflow from the mill was the source of the water that ran under the culvert by Rectory Cottages.

Later, Rectory was farmed by John Eveleigh. We were very impressed as he had been to university and won a rowing blue, he had an oar hanging in the mill barn. Later he also gave me permission to shoot over his farm.

Farther on the lane forked around a small triangle of young fir trees where Mistle Thrushes and Song Thrushes used to nest. A lady later had a wooden garage built in the middle of the copse.

Taking the left fork the lane led down to two stone pillars one either side. Over the hedge here to the left was our 'Aeroplane' tree where we used to pretend to do parachute jumps from the branches of an old, sloping, sweet chestnut tree.

In the lane here was also a dry rectangular culvert, running under the lane, through which we used to crawl. On the right much later they built some council houses, but on the left was the start of Rosedene's garden.

In the corner of this garden there was a dump of old tins, which was most useful when we had a school project requiring us to collect as many labels of foodstuffs from around the world as we could. I seem to remember most of our contributions came from this dump.

I was very surprised when I first saw the name Rosedene on this bungalow as it was so close to the name of my first school in Thornton Heath, and pronounced the same.

The first house on the right was Raymond's house. By the entrance to the main road was a large house on the right occupied by two lovely old ladies Miss Nolting and Miss Spriggs. During the war on the left was an ivy covered ruined house, before Charlie Marshall built the new one.

Against the wall of the ruin stood coils of barbed wire, placed there by the Home Guard, to be stretched across the lane and the main road if the Germans invaded Bratton.

The Home Guard took it the guarding of Bratton very seriously and posted sentries every night by Sentry Cross. They used to stand guard with a loaded shotgun until one nearly shot another by accident one night. After that the gun was unloaded. There was also a searchlight based up near Ditchends. The Home Guard were never very happy with us stalking them when they were practising manoeuvres.

At this point also was the village phone box, again a shelter from the rain for us and we never knew whether we would be lucky enough to get a forgotten three pennies, if we pressed Button B. We also used to annoy the operators by dialling 0 and engaging them in stupid conversations.

Next to it was the old Post Office, the function of which was transferred to the Lower Shop just as I came to live in Bratton. This house had a long garden with some very nice tasting apple trees, but this orchard had to be raided after dark, and was a little dangerous, as Harry Prideaux the owner was a bit irascible.

Opposite were the iron railings of the garden of Sunshine Cottages, which ran alongside the only piece of pavement in the village.

The railings extended from the two Sunshine Cottages, which we had bought for my sister to live in and was so named by her, all the way to the field gate by 2 Prospect Place. That was the extent of the gardens of both cottages. I later came to detest these railings as Father had me painting them with aluminium paint every year.

Sunshine Cottages and the Dreaded Railings

Chapter 24

Bratton Fair

Fairfield was a favourite playground of ours being central and flat. We would have bicycle races here, and play football, marking the goals with our coats. The owner of the field, Tony Hill, was one of our friendly farmers so we had no fear of him.

On rainy days the large barn in the field was a favourite retreat. Usually there were a few bales of hay to sit on. Behind was an open shed which housed the haymaking machinery and we played for hours on that.

I always compared this barn to the one mentioned in the 'William' books, and in fact at one time wondered whether Richmal Crompton was Mothers pseudonym, as the books seem to mirror our escapades.

Many of the villages held a sheep fair once a year when farmers would bring their sheep and cattle to a central point in the village for sale. This was normally turned into a fête with stalls and other attractions. Bratton's fair was held on Fairfield in the middle of August.

We boys would start getting excited a few days before when the sheep pens were being erected. These were set in lines and stretched from the northern hedge to the middle of the field running at right angles to the road.

Each pen consisted of three wooden hurdles, hammered into the ground, closed by a fourth left loose but tied to the others with binder twine to form a gate. Each pen would have a coloured and numbered ticket stuck on a hurdle with paste, to identify the owner of the sheep.

Not far inside the field gate from the road was a gate to an adjoining field. In this field the auctioneer would set up a ring, constructed of steel tube, and pens to hold the cattle for sale. These operations were very interesting to us and we assisted, or got in the way of the workers, with great delight.

Even more exciting were the activities the day before the fair. Barnstaple Council owned a large number of professionally made stalls. They were kept in a room under the British Restaurant, at the end of the Pannier Market, and leased out to villages for their fêtes. They would arrive the day before and the erecting of these gaily coloured stalls was a source of wonder to us.

There were Hoopla stalls and ones where you rolled a penny down a slotted wooden slope trying to land it exactly in the middle of a marked prize square. Additionally a pole was set up horizontally about six feet off the ground where brawny village youths would sit astride and try to knock each other off with sacks filled with straw.

The skittle alley would be transported down from the Hall and set up behind the barn for 'Bowling for the Pig'.

The tea urns would also come, to be set up on trestle tables in the newly swept barn, for refreshments. On the outside of the barn would be pinned a drawing of a Donkey for blindfolded children to try to pin the tail. These stalls were all erected in the north-west quarter of the field nearest the road.

In the far quarter, the courses for races were laid out, their boundaries marked with sawdust, courtesy of Harold Parkin or Clifford Ley at Loxhore Lane, from their circular saws. There were courses for foot races, slow bicycle, and egg and spoon races.

One race that we boys loved was the obstacle race where one had to climb through old car tyres hung from a pole and under a pegged down tarpaulin, amongst other obstacles. There were other trials of strength for the men, lifting 56lb weights, or hammering a peg to send a striker up to ring a bell.

On the day itself we would arrive in the field in the early hours and help Watts' and Champion's cattle lorry drivers to unload the sheep and cattle and drive them into the pens.

I vividly remember helping John Watts' son who in later years sent his lorries, driven by Jack Bawden, to my farm to take my bullocks to South Molton market. Many local farmers would drive their own cattle to the field through the village. Villagers knew that this was one of the few days they had to keep their garden gates shut and you had to be careful where you walked in the road after the animals had passed.

All the village would arrive later with the selling normally starting between nine and ten o'clock. Two auctioneers would be employed, with the cattle and sheep sales progressing concurrently. The cattle salesman would stand on a rostrum near the ring but the sheep salesman would stand on Tony Hill's cart and slowly progress down the lines of pens, selling each in turn.

When we boys had exhausted our pennies on the side shows we would sit on the cart, whilst the horse slowly plodded its way down the lines, stopping at each pen, listening to the fast, and to the unpractised ear, unintelligible, auctioneers patter. We were always fascinated by the speed of his speech but understood it better than the evacuees who were amazed at the livestock sales.

Lunches and teas were served by the ladies in the barn where the tables groaned with homemade produce. Split Rounds, which were small bread buns baked by George Ewens and split to be filled with clotted cream and homemade strawberry jam. There were all kinds of cakes and current buns, pasties, sandwiches and oceans of tea from the urns, the water being boiled in large kettles on a wood burning stove imported to the barn for the purpose.

It would be a replete and happy village that wended its way home in the early evening to get changed for the dance in the Hall that always followed. In the case of the farming menfolk the dance would be preceded by a session in the White Hart to talk over the sales and purchases of the day.

I understand that the holding of a cattle fair bestowed the status of a 'Town' on a community. That would account for the naming of Town Farm, although I always understood it to be so called because it was the nearest to Barnstaple.

Chapter 25

Village Personalities

The most common names in the village were Hill and Heal pronounced the same. Mother used to say that you would be right most of the time if you greeted anyone with this.

Art Heal's Son Leslie and Janet Cockbill's Wedding
A lot of Heals

At that time Bratton was much smaller than the village of today. Now it has become a development dormitory town for Barnstaple it is doubtful if any resident knows the name of everybody living there.

Then though, everybody knew

everybody by name, including the children. If sighted we were never incognito, like today's youth, but would be recognised from a great distance. Equally we would recognise our elders and know whom to give a wide berth.

There were certain ones however that we tormented the life from, as we could run faster than them. One of these was Dickie Jones and we often referred to him as Dickie to his face, which infuriated the little man. Gerald Ley, prompted by us, one day passing Dickie Jones in the road said "Good morning Dickie".

Unfortunately for him he was a little too close and Dickie grabbed him and sat him in the gutter, giving him a cuff into the bargain and saying "It's Mr Jones to you boy, and don't you forget it". Gerald arose with soaking trousers but I think it imprinted the correct mode of address on his memory. There was no ban on corporal punishment by any adult in those days, so it would have been no good him complaining.

Dickie used to shear our sheep for us. He did not have the use of a shearing machine as I did when I sheared my own in later years. He would gather them outside the paddock gate in Craigside drive and set to with a pair of hand shears. He made a far neater job with these than I ever did with my machine, albeit with the expenditure of much more effort.

It's funny how fashions change over the years. At one time all farmers and farm workers wore not only hobnail boots but also stiff leather leggings, they had two pairs, one black and scruffy for everyday wear and the other brown and highly polished, to wear on market days or Sundays.

These, with corduroy breeches, were almost a uniform. Nowadays it is Wellingtons and anything, even jeans, I have not seen a pair of leggings for years. I believe the last farm worker in Bratton to retain this style of dress was Jack Folkes who inhabited one of the Alms houses in later life.

Watty Holmes could always be seen walking through the village carrying a tool of some sort ranging from a pitchfork, to an Old Father Time scythe over his shoulder, on his way to work on one of the farms. He was a very genial fellow and very friendly to all except his neighbour Dickie Jones. Why they fell out I have no idea but they never exchanged even a "Good Morning" all the time I knew them.

With the coming of electricity I remember Watty saying, "Tiz wonderful we can zee much later to light the oil lamp now".

He would insist on not only turning off the main switch before retiring each night but also make sure there was a plug in each socket, "In case that 'lectric leaks out".

I always got on well with Watty except for one time. We boys were watching him build a brick barn behind his house next to Craigside hedge where we had taken up a vantage point. He playfully flicked water over us from his bucket with a trowel. I entered into the spirit of the game by finding a rusty tin full of water on the hedge top and pouring it over his head.

Pat says he will never forget the water running around the brim of Watty's old trilby and falling in a curtain over his face. I will never forget his roar of rage and his close pursuit waving his trowel.

I made good my escape but Mother, coming out to see what all the noise about was greeted by an irate Watty saying, "Look what Master David has done to me". When I arrived home I escaped a severe wigging by telling her that Watty had started throwing water first, but Watty was rather cool towards me for a few days.

I think it was not long after this that he chased us out of his field and had us clambering back over the hedge into

Craigside paddock. We climbed the hedge via a pile of tree trunks which he had felled, trimmed, and leaned against the hedge. The trimming process left sharp spikes and Pat slipped onto one getting a very nasty gash in his inner thigh.

He arrived in the paddock spouting blood from it. I rushed him to our back door and shouted to my mother who was upstairs, "Can Pat come in Mummy, but he will make a mess, he is bleeding all over the place".

Mother came hurtling down stairs and applied a compress covered in her favourite remedy, Dettol. Pat was taken into North Devon Infirmary for stitches and still bears the scar.

At the bottom of the village lived Mrs. Sugden and her daughter Rosemary who were evacuees. I believe Mrs. Sugden was the first president of Bratton WI. One day some soldiers were passing through the village and she invited them in for a cup of tea.

In return they presented her with a large quantity of chocolate, of which she and Rosemary made short work. Unfortunately the next day they discovered that the 'chocolate' had been Exlax and they were confined to barracks for a few days.

Another frequent visitor to the village

was Mr. Singh, a foreign gentleman who wore a turban. I remember my mother keeping me indoors when he came through. For some reason she had the idea that foreign people stole children. I would have thought she would have been pleased to get rid of me.

Having cycled from Barnstaple he would sell small items of linen. He was a friendly man and Laurie's mother would revive him, after his ride, with a cup of tea.

One item he sold was a large, red, spotted handkerchief, one of which the vicar bought and caused a certain amount of amusement when he used it during his sermon. The church resounded to a foghorn blast with his face totally obscured in this large, red spotted kerchief.

In the bungalow Rosedene, in Vicarage Lane, lived two ladies. Mrs Ross-Esson and Miss Broad. Mrs Ross-Esson was very pretty, petite and wore very feminine clothes. Miss Broad was tall, had a short masculine haircut and wore suits with trousers, the only lady to wear trousers in Bratton in that time.

This provided us boys, and I believe, the rest of the village with much speculation. I do not think the village was ready to accept twenty first century morals at that time. The word 'gay' was frequently used but in an entirely different connotation. They were, however a charming couple.

Old Charlie Clarke lived at the bottom of the village, his son Young Charlie, with his wife, lived in a house on the corner of Beara Lane, behind Mrs Tucker's, opposite Lower Chapel. Young Charlie had two daughters Iris and Phyllis.

Young Charlie did part time work on farms but was more usually to be found leaning against Mrs Clarke's garden wall at the entrance to Beara Lane with his dog at his feet. Most of his work was done early morning or night for he was reputedly the best trapper, and it was rumoured, the best poacher, for miles around.

Old Charlie was a very portly and impressive personality. He always sat by the entrance door in the Hall when any function was held and collected entrance fees, and frequently refused us admission to certain events as he considered us troublemakers. We usually evaded him though and sneaked in a back way. He was also a staunch whist drive supporter.

Charlie claimed to know all about explosives, as he had been in the Great War, so when a firework display was organised at the end of the second war he took charge.

Charlie had all the fireworks in a cardboard box and somehow a wayward cracker landed in the box. There was pandemonium as rockets hurled in all directions and the whole event was spectacularly completed in a few seconds. Charlie was not popular, but nobody was really surprised, nor was anyone injured.

A slight problem arose later with Charlie when the village postmen were replaced with ones from Barnstaple. There were two of them, one doing the top half and the other the lower half of the village.

Whereas the local postmen knew everybody by name, the new ones delivered by address, and houses that had never displayed a name were forced to erect signs.

For a few weeks we received no post at The Cottage. On querying this we found that it was all going to Charlie whose house was also called The Cottage and he never passed our mail on. It emerged that his cottage pre-dated ours and should have been called The Old Cottage, but to avoid confusion we had all our future mail addressed to, The Cottage on the Hill.

Mr Murch was a welcome visitor to the village. He would arrive at the bottom of the village and park his Traction Engine and

Thresher in the road outside Town Farm one evening.

We would cycle down to view this monster with the steam hissing forth as it stood in all its splendour. It had a nameplate proclaiming it to be 'Pride of the West'. Next day we would be up early to see it reversing into the yard next to the straw stack. The threshing machine would be connected to the large flywheel of the engine by a belt.

Two men would mount the thresher and one on top of the rick would start to throw sheaves of corn down to them. One man would cut the binder cord from the sheaves and throw them into the gaping maw of the thresher whilst the other would shake them loose with a pitchfork.

Two more men would be employed to carry the threshed ears of corn, which were deposited in sacks attached to the rear of the thresher, into the granary. Out of the side of the thresher would be blown the chaff or 'douse', as it was called, which formed into a great heap.

The threshed straw would appear out of the front of the machine, retied in sheaves. These sheaves would be carried away to make a new straw stack, and eventually be used as bedding.

Mr Murch spent his time fussing around the engine regulating its speed and feeding the fire with coal and the boiler with water. Although we could only watch this activity we were enthralled with the noise and the steam, our only use being to chase the rats that emerged from the base of the rick, with our sticks.

We used to follow Mr Murch's progress from farm to farm, until he completed the work at Mr Thorne's, Beara.

Mr Vickery, who farmed Town Tenement, was another of our friendly farmers who never minded us playing on his land or in fact in his barns. His land stretched below Craigside field, in one of his fields was a disused quarry. It was here we would gather to smoke illicitly bought cigarettes or light fires.

The Home Guard also used this quarry as a rifle range and we would spend hours digging the spent lead bullets from behind the target area. At the bottom of the field it adjoined Fanshawes' ground and on the hedge grew one Horse Chestnut tree and several Sweet Chestnut trees. These provided us with our conkers and the chestnuts to roast in front of the fire at Christmas.

I think Farmer Vickery was

understandably surprised one day to open his door and find four small boys clutching various dusty old musical instruments they had found in a loft over his barn. They had the cheek to ask him, if he had finished with them, could they have them to start a band! He merely said he had not finished with them and would they kindly replace them where they had found them.

Jim Skinner lived just above Sentry Cross. He had a son Alec, who trained as a mechanical engineer. Jim used to drive a lorry and we would hang on the back and run with it until it went too fast and then our feet only touched the ground now and again. Extremely dangerous, and even more so because Jim didn't know we were doing it.

Jim had trouble with his 'esses' and the word 'sit' came out as 'shit' much to the amusement of small minds. Unkind folks would always try to get Jim to say 'sit' when on the bus or in the Village Hall.

Jim was a nice man and very clever, as were all the Skinners. When I worked in a Design Drawing Office he gave me a set of instruments that had belonged to Alec. Not only did I use them for the four years I was a draughtsman but still have them and use them now.

Farmer Skinner lived in 'The Valley of Succour', a farm on the opposite side of Benton Road and kept some bullocks in a field down the village. He used to carry a bale of hay to them accompanied by his dog Bounce. He wore an old leather flying helmet and wire framed glasses, and according to Laurie, looked like Emperor Hirohito.

One snowy day, as they were passing the White Hart, Laurie, having been dared by the Lott boys, hit him with a well compacted snowball under the left ear, knocking up his helmet and his glasses. He dropped his bale and set off in pursuit shouting for Bounce to "Get him", Bounce just ran in circles barking but Laurie ran into a snowdrift and was caught. He had a sound cuffing but refused to give his name.

Farmer Skinner was mightily angry and asked the Lotts the name of the miscreant. To their credit they feigned ignorance, but he went on down the road asking all he met. The incident got to the attention of Sam Bentham who demanded in school that the culprit own up but he also got no response.

Farmer Sid Hill was a brother, I think, to Farmer Bert Hill who lived in the bungalow next to Fairfield. Farmer Sid was tall and always wore a long mackintosh sort of coat with large poacher's pockets. He used to say that he would put us in his pocket if we gave him any trouble, but always in a good-humoured way.

Fred Bale was not only postman and Home Guard Quartermaster but also umpire for the village cricket team. His son, Lionel was away in the army during the war but we anticipated his return with excitement, as he was reputed to be the fastest bowler in the west.

It was rumoured, however, that when Lionel was bowling Fred's hand reached the sky before the cry of "Huzzat" went up on an LBW claim. It was further reported that the same hand appeared to be overcome with laziness when Lionel was batting.

The cricket field itself deserves a mention in that the wicket was levelled out of the sloping outfield. A medium stroke one way would send the ball into the stinging nettles by Rectory Drive, whereas a hard low hit in the other direction would have the ball rebounding off the bank, at the edge of the wicket, to return to the batsman.

Fielders also were not amused at having to collect the ball after it had travelled through a wet cow pat. I remember, on the return to school of West Buckland School team, after a match against Bratton, with their whites liberally bespattered, denying that I had ever heard of the village.

George Carpenter decided to try his hand at chimney sweeping and one of his first customers were the Misses Thompson and Jackson who lived next to Dunkery, behind Sunshine Cottages. He pushed the brush up the chimney screwing on the rods as he progressed until the brush appeared out of the chimney pot.

On pulling it down it stuck, so he reversed his twisting motion with the obvious result that the rods unscrewed leaving the brush somewhere high up in the chimney. How, or if, he ever got it down is not recalled but the ladies could not have a fire for some time.

Fred Ewens was the village practical joker and many of his escapades are recorded elsewhere in this volume. He started very young with his first reported prank landing him in serious trouble. It was in the days of the Barnstaple to Lynton railway.

Fred was watching the trains at Bratton station. These trains had a vacuum braking system, the failure of which caused an immediate application of the brakes. When the train started to move Fred ran alongside it until it had reached a good speed and then he pulled off the vacuum pipe.

The train slammed to a halt depositing all the passengers in heaps at the front of the carriages. Fred was not a popular boy.

Bob Penfold, an old gypsy and horse dealer, who lived in Greenacres at Stowford, was a regular visitor to the White Hart. Other patrons at closing time used to load him onto his horse, which had been patiently waiting outside. They would then give it a slap on the rump and it would take him home with no assistance from Bob. His wife never settled in the house so they moved back into a Romany caravan, but later moved again into the centre of the village.

I cannot leave this chapter on personalities without mentioning my father. He was the kindest and most generous man I ever knew.

He was sought out by villagers on numerous occasions, for advice or financial assistance and they never left empty handed. He gave me two rules which I have tried to obey. Firstly, do not lend anything, including money, if you cannot afford to give it away. Secondly, never ask for the return of anything, including money, you have loaned someone.

He would not thank me for revealing specific actions so I will confine myself to mentioning two already in the public domain.

It is little known that he organised and to a large extent funded the School party from as early as 1940. He never sat at the Heads table for the meal but he and my mother could be found in the kitchens washing up. He also instigated and paid for the Savings stamps given as a present to each child, after the war replacing them with a gift of money.

He later financed a Trust Fund to ensure the children of Bratton would have a Christmas Party in perpetuity and wished, if the school ever closed, that the parties should still continue in the village.

Even after the Trust Fund was established he still provided the tea, sugar, bread and the milk etc. himself. He attended every party until his death, and after he became blind and could no longer assist with the washing up he would sit by the stove and ask me if all the children were enjoying themselves, and how their homemade party hats looked.

When electricity first came to Bratton we were one of the few households to possess a television. For the coronation in 1953 he went into Barnstaple and purchased a long aerial lead. He positioned our TV in the Chapel with the lead running up the road to our aerial. This allowed the whole village to witness the event and the Chapel was full all day.

Mother and Father

Chapter 26

Excursions

One outing we never missed was to Barnstaple Fair, held in September. We would eagerly await this momentous event and on the Saturday before, after we had visited the Gaumont, we would go round to the County Garage via North Walk to see how the preparations had progressed.

On the evening of our visit to the fair we would get off the bus in the Strand and immediately be assailed by the noise of the steam organs, and would see the bright lights ahead.

The sideshows started opposite Queen Anne's Walk and the first one was usually a Strong Man. He would be bending iron bars in his hands or by beating them over his left bicep. His arm was much bruised, I remember, but he would offer these bent bars to the brawny farm youths who could never bend them straight.

We would work our way from there through the fairground that covered the river bank and road as far as the small bridge. The Chairoplanes, Waltzer, Caterpillar, Bumping and Racing Car rides were all sampled with enthusiasm, as were the stalls with Candy Floss and Shooting Galleries. I remember one year we boys snuck under the canvas into the Nude Show tent which was labelled 'No admittance under 16 years of age'.

We were quite disappointed though, as the maiden danced clothed, albeit fairly scantily, until the end after which the lights were extinguished. When they came on again a fine mesh net had been lowered across the stage and a backlight revealed the motionless, naked maiden behind it in an artistic pose until the light was dowsed again after thirty seconds. We were glad we had not paid.

After sampling all the delights, including the 'Sawing a Lady in Half', The Bearded Lady, The Dwarf and the Fat Lady, all not very PC these days, we would be collected by our parents for the ride home, but the experience would be the major topic of conversation for days.

We would often pack haversacks with sandwiches or Yeast cake and a bottle of pop and walk out to other villages. Challacombe, Stoke Rivers, Shirwell, and Loxhore being the more usual ones. We would always visit them when they had a fête, but at other times go to visit one of our relations who lived there, or in the case of Loxhore, to play with John Dinnicombe, before he moved to Bratton.

We would not always reach our destination as there would be many distractions found along the way, a bird's nest, a stream that needed damming or fishing, or some other diversion but we would return home tired and hungry at nightfall.

Nowadays I expect parents would be horrified at the thought of their five or six year olds disappearing by themselves all day. Ours never knew where we were from morn 'till night but never worried, and we never came to harm.

When my father used to travel to Salisbury, Bournemouth, Weston-super- Mare etc. during the school holidays, I was expected to accompany him but although the seaside resorts were enjoyable I hated the car journeys, and missed my friends.

When he visited Minehead it was normally only a day trip so I always asked if the other three could come. There was not much to do there, in the latter days of the war, the beach was blocked by barbed wire, and the access slopes with large concrete cones, to forestall possible enemy landings.

The only amusement on the front was a machine for stamping names into aluminium labels, and we soon exhausted the delights of that. There was, however, one big bonus on the trip in the last days of the war. An ice cream parlour had opened on the front. Mother always took us in there and ordered us Knickerbockerglories.

These were a mixture of various ice cream and fruits, in an immensely tall conical glass. The first visit was the only one where Laurie had this as he was rather sick on the way home. After that Mother determined he should be restricted to simpler fare.

I accompanied my father one lunch time to the British Restaurant at the end of Butchers Row in Barnstaple. These restaurants were established during the war so that despite rationing people could obtain a cheap nourishing meal. You paid a fixed sum for a meal in them and were given different coloured plastic discs which could be exchanged for a soup, main or sweet course.

My father chose a steak and was surprised at the size and thickness of it. He said it was quite tender but had a bit of a strange fishy taste. I pointed to a board that said, "Today's Special, Whale Steak". Father pushed his plate aside and we left the restaurant before I had time to sample the sweet course. He was very conservative in his tastes.

In 1945, after VE day, my parents arranged for Pat and myself to visit my pre-war home in Thornton Heath, staying with their old neighbours Mr and Mrs Dickson. We were put on the train at Barnstaple Junction and had to change trains at Taunton, being met by Mrs Dickson at Paddington.

The journey was an adventure in itself and we must have annoyed the other passengers chasing up and down the corridor of the London train after Taunton. On the part of the journey prior to that the Barnstaple train had no corridor. I had forgotten much about London life, and the sights, but Pat was even more amazed, never having left Devon before.

The red double-decker buses, the trams and trolley buses intrigued us, as did the dress of the inhabitants. I remember Pat remarking on the long red painted nails of a lady on one of the bus trips saying "Cor, look at her talons".

We rode on the underground and visited many museums, which were just reopening after the war, particularly liking the Science Museum which, among other spectator operated machines, possessed an X-ray machine in which you could place your hand and see your skeleton. I remember a shoe shop in Barnstaple also had one where you could see the fit of your shoes, that was before it was realised how dangerous X-rays are.

We were taken to a Lyons Corner House one day for lunch. I believe this chain of cafés no longer exists. Pat and I were confronted by an extensive menu but both chose Welsh Rarebit, which, because of cheese rationing we had never tasted. I remember Mrs. Dickson being horrified at our choice saying it would mainly consist of Soya flour, but we enjoyed it.

Mr Dickson worked at The Daily Mirror, and it was there he made the copper plate sign for The Cottage which is still on display today, although now covered in paint.

He was a dedicated pianist. One day towards the end of our visit he insisted that Pat and I sit and hear him play classical music all morning. I am sure this was good for our souls but was certainly not our cup of tea, and a lot of fidgeting went on. Despite the unusual spectacles abounding in the city I think we were both very pleased to return to the green green fields of home.

Chapter 27

Guns

Possibly because there was an armed conflict going on at the time, perhaps because of our diet of cowboy films, or maybe it is common to all boys, but we were certainly fascinated by guns.

I used to love playing with my brother's .45 Service revolver when he was home on leave, and was allowed to take it out in the garden. My young fingers were not strong enough to fire the empty pistol through the action but could produce a satisfying click after having first cocked it.

Buster also acquired a .38 revolver from somewhere and spent hours filing out the chambers to take 9mm shotgun cartridges, luckily there being none of the correct ammunition available. I do not know whether he ever completed the task. However we graduated from cap pistols at a relatively early age.

I got my first air rifle when I was about eight years old. It was a Daisy made to fire BB shot but as that was unobtainable I used .177 slugs. Originally I was forbidden to take it out of the back yard and we boys would have shooting competitions at a target pinned on the door of the outside privy. It received so much use that it did not last long and was replaced in short order by first a Milbro rifle and then a BSA .177.

About this time Buster was given a Diana .177 pistol and Laurie inherited his brothers air rifle. Although like me Laurie was originally restricted in its use to his rear garden, where we used to lean on the wall and shoot sparrows off the neighbour's clothes line, this restriction was soon lifted.

I purchased a more powerful BSA .22 from Mr Karneivicz at Haxton cottage and thus equipped, with Pat having the old BSA, we terrorised the neighbourhood.

The sight today of four small boys carrying guns through the village would probably cause the summoning of the Armed Response Unit of the Police. In those days it was thought nothing of. All farmers and farm workers had shotguns which were carelessly left standing in unlocked barns for anyone to take.

The total extent of any legislation was for shotguns, and for these the only requirement was to visit the Village Post Office and, for five shillings (25p), purchase a Gun Licence, for which there was no lower age limit. When I bought my first shotgun, a 9mm bolt action Garden Gun from George Carpenter for £3, at the tender age of ten, I purchased a licence. There was no problem for me to buy cartridges for it in Barnstaple at Gales, they would not even ask if I had a licence.

This shotgun was the cause of one of our only three accidents with guns, all three being caused by faulty guns. On the first day I had it we left George Carpenters and went down to Button River. We were so enamoured of it that we all took turns in carrying it for short periods, loaded of course in case we saw a rabbit.

When we came to cross the river under Tidicombe Cleave balancing on stones, Pat was behind me carrying the gun. He stumbled and the gun went off, the shot entering the water just behind my heels. He swore that he had never touched the trigger.

We later found that the trigger mechanism was faulty and in a dangerous state. I remember Rex was home at the time and he took it into Gales who repaired it, and also replaced the missing extractor.

Our second lucky escape was when I was twelve and had acquired my first twelve bore. This was a very old single barrel hammer gun and the safety was the half cock position. With the hammer in this position it should not be possible to fire it but Buster was quite strong and one day testing it, with a great deal of muscle applied, he managed to do so, narrowly missing Laurie who a few moments before had been standing in front of the barrel. Again this gun immediately went to Gales for repair.

We must have had a very conscientious Guardian Angel watching over us boys as, apart from these two narrow escapes, the only damage we ever inflicted on anyone was the self administered pellet in my cheek, which was also occasioned by a faulty gun in that it had lost its trigger guard.

I was lucky on that occasion the wound did not turn septic. I did worry for a while about lead poisoning, but as the pellet has been in my cheek now for over sixty years, I think the danger of that has passed.

The ancient twelve bore in question was later de-activated by the Birmingham Proof House for me, after I acquired a double barrel gun, and hangs on my landing wall today.

We seldom went out, from then on, without carrying at least one gun and more often one each. Our favourite targets in the village, with the airguns, were the school bell and Fred Ewen's windmill. Apart from those we shot at many rabbits over the fields but only the .22 was powerful enough to do them any damage.

The only birds to fall victim were the occasional innocent sparrow and the not so innocent crows and rooks, especially those in lower Rectory Drive. I do remember one lucky shot netting us a rabbit when sighted from high up on one side of Beara Cleave and it was sitting across the valley sunning itself. I could not believe that I had hit it but Curly Barrow proved it by running down the slope, and up the other side collecting it from outside its burrow.

We also used to visit the stone bed of the old railway line, a favourite haunt in the sun for vipers. I do not remember us ever being quick enough to shoot one, our sticks were a much more effective weapon against them.

After a while we found the Garden Gun to be ineffective against rabbits with its shot cartridges containing so few and such small size of shot, that its effective range was only about ten yards. We overcame this by casting solid lead bullets.

We melted lead with a blowtorch and

poured it into sand moulds, replacing the shot in the paper cartridges with these. Due to the smooth bore of the gun it was rather inaccurate but gave a much greater range and effectiveness, although probably highly illegal.

If the old oak bench is still lying on its side, somewhere in the Pleasure Field at the top of the village, there may be found several of these homemade bullets embedded in it, attesting to the increased power, as this was our testing ground.

I would say that, although at that time we had easy access to guns, and every schoolboy carried a knife, I never heard of anyone using either to attack anybody. This contrasts with the horrendous newspaper reports of today. Nobody to my recollection ever sustained a deliberate injury.

Chapter 28

Odds and Ends

It is thought that arranged marriages and having ones spouse picked by the family is something occurring only in the East but it seemed to be true in our village also. When I was five I got engaged to Margaret Marshall and we exchanged curtain rings. A few days later I was jumped on by her brother Derek, soundly thrashed and my 'ring' taken. He said how dare I get engaged to his sister without his permission, she got the same treatment so we called it off.

When I was young my mother though it was good discipline to make me assist with the household chores, so I was set various tasks on days when there was no school. She was very strict about this, and although she despaired of my efforts at dusting a room, which she checked by wiping her white handkerchief over all exposed surfaces, she found other work which she felt more suited to my talents.

I would be locked into the wash house in the morning on some days, with orders to chop up a faggot of kindling, and a large saucepan to be filled with chopped old potatoes, which would be boiled and mixed with corn meal for the poultry.

She would leave the key on the window-sill outside the wash house. I would soon hear my friends come into the backyard to call for me.

In those times, house doors were never locked, hardly anyone used their front door except those houses that had a very difficult rear access, such as terraced cottages. For example I would never have dreamed of knocking at Laurie's front door until years after he had left home and I visited his mother. It was just not done. I suppose it may have been that most front doors led directly into the front room which was never entered except on high days and holidays.

Anyway on hearing their arrival I would call out and they would unlock the door and come in. They would all set to with a will and my work would be finished in no time. They would then go out, relock the door and replace the key, knock on the back door and ask my mother if I could come out to play.

She would come to see if I had finished my chores and be rather surprised at the neat pile of kindling and saucepan of neatly chopped potatoes. I think she must have had an inkling what had happened but never let on. She would reward us all with a glass of skimmed milk and a slice of Yeast cake which they much appreciated.

Other times I would have been set the task of washing up the breakfast utensils for our family of five. The gang would arrive and we had a set routine for this task. Buster would wash, Pat would wipe, while I would sit on the kitchen table and supervise, telling Laurie in which cupboard to put everything!

They never seemed to mind doing all the work while I did nothing, they were very loyal friends and still are. Obviously I was destined to be an officer rather than a worker! Pat remembers a frequent visitor to my house, Jim Smith, on leave from the Merchant Navy, teaching him a quicker method of wiping several plates at once. He says he still thinks of it now when he is helping his wife.

One day, when we four were in the wash house we came upon the tins of raddle and oil used for marking the sheep. These were tins of red, blue, green and black powder which, when mixed with the oil formed a paint. This paint was applied daily to the ram's chest when it was tupping time (time for the ram to be put with the ewes). This way the ram would mark the ewes backs, when he served them, and my father could tell which ewes had been served and, by changing the colour each week, when they had been.

We mixed all the colours with the oil and finding some brushes proceeded to paint various parts of the paddock with different colour splashes. I then thought of the nice big area of the galvanised pig sty roof which I thought could do with extra paint protection so the four of us climbed up and took a quarter each and set to work.

It exhausted my father's total supply of raddle but he never knew where the bulk of it went. However, in later years when I flew over the village I never had any trouble about picking out Craigside as the multicolour roof stood out boldly from the air. It was a good testimony to the lasting and protective properties of our paint that it was still bright after more than twelve years.

The few splashes that my father noticed made him think that the tins must have been nearly empty so we did not get into very hot water, but I think our mothers must have noticed some varied hues on our clothes.

An open gutter ran down the side of the main road. I think the flow originated from the spring above Castle Cottages where the Yendells lived with their daughter Betty. The flow was quite pure, and only piped under house entrances and the pavement past Sunshine Cottages. We children used to sail toy boats down the gutter and play Pooh Sticks through the pipes.

My friends would not lend me their comics after Mother burnt the first ones she caught me reading. She classed the Beano, Dandy and Radio Fun as 'Penny Dreadfuls' and would not allow them in the house so I had to read them at the other houses. She relented later over 'The Champion' and I was able to read 'Rockfist Rogan of the RAF', stories over and over again.

After we lost our first sheepdog, Bruce, we acquired a Welsh Collie of dubious temperament. Mother used to keep him chained in the barn and push his meals towards him with a stick whilst he growled and snapped. His sole redemption was that he was good with sheep.

He was also good with me, and I had no fear of him, but always kept him on a lead. One Sunday after our walk Mother gave me a bucket of food for him and I fed him in the back yard. A crust of bread fell out of the bucket and I picked it up and threw it back in whilst he was eating. He growled at me so I stamped my foot at him, next thing I knew I was on the ground with him on top.

Father rescued me but a trip to North Devon Infirmary resulted in thirteen stitches in my face and I was lucky not to have lost an eye. Bill Bale despatched the dog that night but my face presented a sorry sight. During my enforced confinement for recovery I think every child in the village visited me, such a close knit community we were then, and I was inundated with gifts of books and jigsaws.

There was a shed at the end of Laurie's garden above the Trap house. Bill Merrett kept his beehives just outside the shed and we used to watch him smoking the bees before opening the hives and extracting the honey combs. He did not have a honey extractor but when my mother received a comb she would slice the wax off and stand it to drain in a bowl. It was a very welcome addition to the sugar ration.

Outside the shed George kept Guinea Pigs for which he used to send us on excursions to collect dandelion leaves. This was a dangerous occupation, as we knew if you got the milky sap on your hands you would wet the bed! George used to say that if you held a Guinea Pig up by its tail its eyes would drop out, it was a long time before I understood why. George was later to rebuild a racing bicycle in the shed.

George on his racing bike
Note hay cart lades in background

We often saw farmers ploughing and haymaking with horses although there were quite a few Petrol/TVO tractors starting to appear. I remember the first Ferguson grey tractor arriving in the village but cannot remember which affluent farmer purchased it.

I also saw one Field Marshall Diesel, normally parked in the quarry opposite Quarry House, which had to be started by the insertion of a piece of burning paper into the cylinders. There was a Fordson kept in Cart Linhay on which we used to play.

Farming then, besides being at subsistence level, was much more physical than today. There were no manure spinners, no muck spreaders and no fore end loaders, besides artificial fertilizer being unobtainable it would still have been unaffordable.

Every day during the winter when the cattle were kept indoors, to avoid them poaching the wet fields with their hooves, the shippons had to be cleaned. Dung, mixed with bedding straw was cleared from the shippons by hand with a fork and wheelbarrow and piled in a steaming heap nearby. This heap became mountainous over the winter even with a small number of cattle.

When spring came, or sometimes even earlier when the ground was hard with frost, this well rotted manure was spread on the fields. As there was no mechanical assistance it was back to the dung fork, with long curved tines and heave it from the heap into the 'Butt'. This was a small cart with high sides.

The farmer would then get up on the shafts and drive the horse and butt to the field where he would take up position, standing on top of the load. He would throw down a goodly heap of dung before commanding the horse to "Walk on", from his perch on top of the load.

This was not without its dangers as, if the horse started with a jerk and the farmer had not braced himself well with his fork, he could find himself deposited in the pile he had just thrown down.

Just such an incident happened later when Laurie was first driving a tractor in similar circumstances with Farmer Smallridge on the cart. Letting in the clutch too quick he deposited his employer head first into a steaming heap. Luckily for Laurie, Farmer Smallridge had a sense of humour and the lad kept his job.

The farmer would bid the horse to "Whoa" after some yards and repeat the process. The field would eventually be covered with lines of small dung heaps. Dismounting, the farmer would have then to spread the heaps, throwing forkfuls in all directions so that the field was evenly covered. It is much quicker and a lot less effort to write this than to do the job, which I have done myself, albeit single handed, with a tractor before I could afford a spreader.

It would take many returns to the main dung heap to refill the butt, even to cover a relatively small field, and could take days to do what a modern dung spreader and tractor can accomplish in a morning.

This time consuming expenditure of effort also applied to other horse powered jobs such as ploughing. Walking behind a horse drawn, one or two furrow plough all day was far less productive than sitting on a multi horse power tractor pulling a six furrow plough.

We quickly realised that, when we first saw tractors arriving in Bratton, the demise of the cart horse, although sad in a way, was going to be swift and inevitable. I think that today's farm workers, sitting in their padded tractor cabs, with headphones listening to Radio One would not change places with their predecessors on top of a dung butt.

When we had been upset by a particular farm worker, and even sometimes when they were innocent of deserving our wrath, we would play a dirty trick on them. Most farmers gathered their sheep against a field gate and, while they were held there by the dog, would perform such tasks as foot trimming or dagging.

Because of this they used to leave a bottle of sheep dip in the hedge beside the gate to wash out any maggots. We would sometimes find the farmers lunch, also concealed in the hedge, which contained a bottle of cold tea, and swap the tea for the dip, as they looked so similar. They did not smell or taste the same though!

The vicar Rev. Cave-Moyle had a grey Standard eight car. Mounted on the radiator cap was a chromium effigy of a monkey with its hands to its nose making a rude gesture to oncoming traffic. Whenever we came across the parked car we would always turn the monkey around so that it was gesturing to the vicar through the windscreen. This would occasion rather irreverent language on the vicar's return, as he repositioned it, before driving off in a fury.

When Rev. Cave-Moyle left the Vicarage, there was a sale of household effects to clear it. It then stood empty for a long period, the new incumbent, Rev. Gover, went to live down Station Road in Bragan House which became the new Rectory. After the sale the auctioneers, whilst securing the doors of the empty house, carelessly left an upstairs window open.

This was an open invitation to us and we lost no time in exploring this hitherto forbidden domain. We were amazed at the very extensive wine cellars with all the stone wine racks, I think they must have held a lot more than communion wine in their time. Outside there was a shed containing a very large generator that must, at one time, have supplied the house with electric light.

In 1944 many American troops were encamped around the fringes of Exmoor in the build up to D day. We had quite an increase of traffic through the village because of this with many lorries and armoured vehicles. We would run behind the troop lorries shouting, "Got any gum chum?" The GIs would normally shout back "Yes mister, got a sister?" This response would normally be accompanied by a few packets of Spearmint being thrown to us.

I believe that this increase of traffic only resulted in one serious accident. This occurred when a Sherman tank, on its way down the Turnpike, went over the edge of the road opposite Oxenpark and rolled down the cleave towards Chumhill. It was recovered later but I think the occupants were badly injured.

At the end of the war you could buy

plastic covered wire in Barnstaple in red, green, blue or white. We used to weave multi-coloured bracelets and rings out of this and sell them to a craft shop in Joy Street, Barum. We also used to make brooches out of fuse wire.

Chapter 29

Sam's or Top Class

School today minus bell. Shot off?

It was in 1945 that they brought in the eleven plus, I believe that until then it was called a Scholarship. Pat, Raymond and I were among the second group to take it in 1946. In 1945 the first of the new scholarships were won by pupils of the school, to the Grammar school in Barnstaple.

My previous mentor Kathleen Shapland from Stoke, Gordon Lott and Joyce Sturman from Bratton Mill won the first. Over the classroom door there was an Honours Board bearing the names of Scholarship winners that had not had any additions for many years. These three names were added, but I believe they were the last as so many pupils passed the 'Eleven Plus' in future years.

I and my friends progressed therefore into a much depleted top form, albeit of a large age range. The reason for this was that all the eleven year olds were removed to the Grammar school if they had passed the exam, and to the Secondary Modern, also in Barnstaple, if they had failed.

Those over the age for the exam were to remain at the school until they left at fourteen, although about this time the leaving age was raised to 15. I believe that some of the older ones went to the Grammar, Technical or Secondary Modern in this transitional period purely on the Heads evaluation.

It was here I met up again with the love of my life at the time, Margaret Marshall. We sat next to each other but separated by an aisle, as Sam had the single desks formed into rows rather than the two seater desks we had in the previous class.

We were soon in trouble as she whispered to me that her mother, Eva, had given birth to a daughter. I whispered back asking her name. She said Janice and kept repeating it, as I kept mishearing it as Janet, so eventually she wrote it down and passed me a note. Unfortunately Sam looked up at that moment and she was in big trouble.

Margaret left the school soon after as she was a year older than me. Our last tryst together was in 1946, after my sisters wedding, when we followed the honeymoon car on our bicycles to Barn Hill. She asked me to marry her then, and I agreed. I went away to boarding school after that and our paths diverged.

I was very unhappy when I heard she had married someone else at sixteen. However I soon fell hopelessly in love with my next door neighbour Janet Bowden, but that is another story.

In this classroom we had a big poster on the wall showing coloured pictures of all types of anti personnel bombs that we might find, and telling us not to touch them. They looked very pretty with their red and yellow bands of colour. I think we were very disappointed, but also very lucky, that we never found any.

One day an army officer came to the school and gave us a talk, requesting that we collect books for soldiers and prisoners of war. He gave us badges of rank as privates and said according to the number of books collected we could rise through the ranks to Field Marshal. We visited all the houses and farms far and wide and collected some very peculiar and ancient books. I'm sure the soldiers would never have read them.

At this time my father was travelling more as his area expanded, and my mother accompanied him on day trips to places like Minehead, so I stayed at the school for lunch on these days. The lunches came out from Barnstaple in insulated steel drums and were served out from Sam's desk.

We sat at our desks to eat them and I must admit I found them very palatable. They consisted of a main course and a sweet. I believe we had to take sixpence (about 2p) or was it nine pence as Dinner Money. The charge was means tested and some of the poorer families qualified for free meals. There were a large number of takers, as previously the children from 'out over' had only cold packed sandwiches that were not very sustaining on a cold winters day.

I remember when the first atomic bomb was dropped we had a lesson from Sam on atomic power. He held up a bottle of Quink ink saying that one day whole towns could be powered, for hundreds of years, by an amount of material that could be contained within the bottle. I was most impressed.

He also said that because of the cheap power and the introduction of automation people would have much more leisure time and the problem would be how to gainfully employ this time. This has proved quite true.

He gave us long lectures on finance and the effects of inflation. He explained why the government could not just print more money when they needed it.

He also surprised us by pulling out his silver pocket watch saying that he much preferred it to a gold one. He explained that gold only had an intrinsic value and was a very soft metal that, although not tarnishing, did not have the strength of silver or steel.

So I did remember something of what he tried hard to teach us. I also still felt his cane on occasions but much less often than when I was in the Infants. I think he mellowed during the few years we knew him.

We soon had to start preparing for the exam. Sam gave us homework, both arithmetic and essays. I hated it, and drove my parents to distraction, as they tried to make me do it when I just wanted to be out on a nice evening. My parents were determined that I would pass and so concentrated on giving me at home, the education I avoided in school.

My mother supervised my essays whilst my father endeavoured to assist me, unsuccessfully, with sums. He was not a patient teacher and no matter how hard I tried to understand what he was saying, I was not quick enough to grasp it, and the sessions normally ended with him slamming out of the house in frustration.

On March 27th 1946 an event happened that was to shape the rest of my life. A very surprised Sam told me that I had passed the eleven plus examination. Buster had also passed, but that was expected. Strangely my previous mentor Vera Ridd Jones, whom I considered very clever, was borderline and had to re-sit.

Pat was also a borderline in the exam and took this very hard, no matter how much we tried to buoy him up, however they both passed on the second attempt so we were all set for the Grammar school together, or so we thought. Laurie, being a year younger took the exam the next year and joined the rest at Barnstaple.

8th June, 1946

To-day, as we celebrate victory, I send this personal message to you and all other boys and girls at school. For you have shared in the hardships and dangers of a total war and you have shared no less in the triumph of the Allied Nations.

I know you will always feel proud to belong to a country which was capable of such supreme effort; proud, too, of parents and elder brothers and sisters who by their courage, endurance and enterprise brought victory. May these qualities be yours as you grow up and join in the common effort to establish among the nations of the world unity and peace.

George R.I.

Commemorative Card

In 1946 the village, with the rest of the country, celebrated Victory Day. All the schoolchildren were issued with a commemorative card. I wonder, how many like me still possess them.

Sports were held on Fairfield and although our Prisoners of War had returned home many German POWs were still at Brayford and attended. We held a tug of war match which they won easily, much to the disgust of Dennis Bye who was affronted that they were allowed to attend.

Following the sports there was a celebration tea in the Village Hall with a dance in the evening. This event finally drew a line under the village's wartime activities and the same spirit of camaraderie would not be seen again.

In school I was no more attentive than I ever had been, and the best Sam could say of me in a leaving report was that he had always known me to be honest, in that I always owned up to my misdeeds when questioned. I suppose that is really an accolade in itself, but it spoke nothing of my academic potential.

I had certain premonitions just after the exams when I was taken by my parents to visit Bluecoat school in Barnstaple, Blundell's at

Tiverton, Wellington College and West Buckland School. However as I voiced my extreme dismay at all of them I really thought they would give in and not separate us.

It may have been that together we had been such trouble as children they dreaded the thought of us around as teenagers. The other possibility was that Father had been promoted to supervise all the Ministry of Supply run garages in the South West. This meant that he was away all week and Mother wanted to accompany him, so I had to leave home.

It certainly never occurred to me that they thought a minor Public School education might secure a better future for me than a Grammar school. I think that they were probably right if they thought along those lines though, as supervised prep at WBS, together with the very strict discipline, was exactly what I needed.

However I really hated going away to boarding school and leaving Bratton for such long periods. The only way they could keep me there was to bring me back each Sunday. I would so much rather have gone to the Grammar School with the rest of the gang. The mere thought of us being split up was enough for tears.

In fact my worst fears were well founded. I hated every minute at West Buckland and ran away twice, each time being returned before my absence was noted. I disliked Rugby and Cricket, I did passably well at Cross Country Running and made the school Shooting Eight.

I only really enjoyed the activities in the Army and RAF cadet force, during which I gained a pilots licence and achieved the senior RAF cadet's position in charge of the Flight. In class, I was normally near bottom, and it was only because I needed a minimum of six GCEs with good marks to enter the RAF that I buckled down to work in my last year, and managed to achieve them. If I hated it so much one wonders why I later sent my son there, but that is another story.

It was, however, the end of my childhood in Bratton, although I continued to live there until 1953, and my parents lived there until their deaths. I still have nothing but affection for Bratton and the friends I made and the surrounding countryside despite the many changes. I visit it whenever possible.

Chapter 30

Epilogue

These then were our Salad Days. I hope I have managed to impart some idea of what village life was like then. I hope that I have given some amusement and not revived any sad memories for relatives of those I have mentioned. If I have, I apologise as it was not my intention.

My friends brought up in the cities and towns, find it hard to believe that in the 1940s there were still places like Bratton with no electricity, where many houses had no mains water and used outside earth closets.

It is quite possible that readers by now will be thinking that the youth of today is not as black as it is sometimes painted. Considering the mischief that we boys, and some of our elders who should have known better, got up to in those days they are probably right.

However in the village, shotguns were left lying around and no doors were locked. Burglary was unknown, drugs unheard of, no muggings, rapes or murders, not even malicious assaults.

And what became of the terrible four?

Buster, or at the last to give him his proper name Raymond, was as I have said, partially paralysed with Polio, and unfortunately died relatively young.

Pat, Raymond, Laurie and David
Before our paths diverged

Of the remaining three, we are all now happily retired with middle age children of our own, we being in our seventies. We each served time in Royal Air Force in engineering related positions, Pat and Laurie for four years and five years respectively, and me for sixteen years.

Pat, through his RAF training and an

apprenticeship with a Barnstaple firm, set up in his own business as an Electrician and now lives in retirement in Ilfracombe.

Laurie, like me, had a varied career, working initially for the Forestry Commission then, after his RAF service, again with the Forestry and a short period on a farm, went back to engineering and teaching. He now lives in retirement in Basingstoke.

I served an apprenticeship and worked in engineering prior to a lengthy spell teaching electronics, maths and science in the RAF and in civilian schools, followed by livestock farming. I then went back to engineering, as a licenced aircraft engineer, working and living in Cyprus and am now in retirement there.

Sam would have been proud of us but would not have believed we would all be as successful in life, for I am sure he thought we were born to be hung.

We three still keep in close contact, and also meet up in the Village for a beer at the White Hart and to visit some of our old haunts. We two eldest have had heart by-pass operations and we find some of the hills and walks too much for us now.

We also exist on a diet of sprays and tablets and mine sometimes amount to as many as ten different medications a day. Long gone are the days when we supplemented our diet with Sour-sabs, Underground nuts, Hazel nuts and young Beech leaves, and drank from field streams.

THE END OF AN ERA

List of Photographs